CAUGHT

IN A CAM NET

COMPILED BY
TOM HAMILTON

Grosvenor House
Publishing Limited

All rights reserved
Copyright © Tom Hamilton, 2018

The right of Tom Hamilton to be responsible for the compilation of this
work has been asserted in accordance with Section 78
of the Copyright, Designs and Patents Act 1988

The book cover picture is copyright to Tom Hamilton

This book is published by
Grosvenor House Publishing Ltd
Link House
140 The Broadway, Tolworth, Surrey, KT6 7HT.
www.grosvenorhousepublishing.co.uk

This book is sold subject to the conditions that it shall not, by way of
trade or otherwise, be lent, resold, hired out or otherwise circulated
without the author's or publisher's prior consent in any form of binding or
cover other than that in which it is published and
without a similar condition including this condition being imposed
on the subsequent purchaser.

A CIP record for this book
is available from the British Library

ISBN 978-1-78623-343-1

LIST OF CONTRIBUTORS

Brigadier N Smith
Lieutenant Colonel (Retired) Phil Nunn
Lieutenant Colonel (Retired) Paul Hodgson
Lieutenant Colonel (Retired) John Walker
Lieutenant Colonel (Retired) Tom Hamilton
Captain N. Rudd
Captain G Davidson
Sam Hatlem-Olsen
Bill Stewart
George Moors
Baz King
Andrew "Milly" Milton

CONTENTS

INTRODUCTION

The Germans had invaded Greece. A troop leader was told to go down to a small bridge nearby and blow it up in order to hinder the German advance. When he arrived, he dismounted and started laying the explosives he had with him. A local farmer approached with a shotgun. The troop leader spoke to him and then used the radio to speak to the Commanding Officer for advice.

"Hello 9 (Commanding Officers callsign) this is 31b. There is a farmer here with a shotgun who says he will shoot me if I blow up the bridge."

There was a pause and then the reply,

"Goodbye then."

This anecdote illustrates two things about tank soldiers. A dogged determination to get things done and a sense of humour. Hussars have both in spades.

I spent thirty eight years as an Hussar, firstly as a Queen's Own Hussar (QOH) and then as a Queen's Royal Hussar (QRH). I joined QOH in 1975 and left QRH in 2013. During my time with QOH I frequently came into contact with members of the Queen's Royal Irish Hussars (QRIH) and I know they had the same sense of humour and attitudes.

So much has changed over the years, but the wheel is turning and perhaps we are approaching full circle. The Cold War Years ended with what was possibly the last conventional war we would fight. The QRIH played a major part in the Gulf War of 1991. Queen's Hussars had long been peace keeping in Northern Ireland. The Balkans saw us turn toward peace making. The middle east became a war of insurgency in theatre and terrorism at home, first in Iraq and then, more aggressively in Afghanistan. The Cold War years saw the Hussar as a tank man. No whole fleet management. A tank you kept, were responsible for and "lived". The Hussars have always been able to adapt rapidly. The Balkans resulted in more flexibility and for many Iraq gave us a much greater understanding of Infantry tactics and capabilities. In Afghanistan these lessons were tested, fully, by a competent enemy. At the time of writing, the Regiment has troops in Estonia, on their tanks, providing deterrence to a more aggressive posture by Russia.

The Regiment faces other threats. There are far fewer regiments and therefore fewer tanks. Some would argue the tank is a thing of the past, yet it is to the tank the Army turns when deterrent is required on the ground. The hugely increased capability of the tank only in part makes up for the significantly fewer tanks we now have, some 700 less than when I first became an Hussar. Excellence in the use of the tank, an ability to perform all Infantry tasks and success on the sporting field must be our defence against obscurity.

The soldiers have not changed. They are still the same raw material they were when I joined. They are more likely to ask "why?" and they are competent on highly technical pieces of kit. They are less experienced on tanks because the current operational and fiscal atmosphere means they do not "Live" tanks in the same way as the Cold war warriors did. However, they are hugely adaptable, learn quickly and are the most excellent ambassadors. They carry the standard of their predecessors well.

This compilation seeks to inform the soldier of today about the soldier of yesterday and vice versa. Not the history, although there is some included but the day to day work of the soldier and his environment. What he did or does and how he thinks, and it seeks to show that Hussars are still quietly determined but with a great sense of fun. It has not been "red inked" and is sometimes written in the language of soldiers. Some names have been changed. There may be some errors as many of the stories are, "as remembered" from many years previously however, they all tell the story of the soldiers in a magnificent regiment.

COLD WAR SOLDIERING

The Cold War was a time of expectation. Are the Russians coming? Will the bomb be used? How long will we survive?

Air raid sirens were tested on a weekly basis throughout Germany, there were television programmes about what to do in the event of a nuclear attack (which basically stated where to put your head and what to kiss) and everyone lived with the background fear that another, nuclear war could start at any time.

Europe was divided. Down the middle of Germany was a fence. Mined, wired and covered by machine gun towers with East German guards watching over it. Its purpose was more to keep East Germans in rather than "The West" out. Churchills Iron Curtain. It was patrolled regularly by The NATO allies within their zones of responsibility.

Huge armies faced each other across the Iron Curtain. The Soviet bloc had many hundreds of thousands of troops ready to face off against the American army and other NATO forces that included about 70000 British troops (3 divisions and support troops) and a significant portion of the RAF. The British zone stretched from the Dutch border to the East German border in a belt about 100 miles wide. America had some 250000 troops to the south of the British zone. Near the Dutch border were RAF bases and large logistic and administrative locations and then almost every large town had a garrison. Dortmund, Soest, Celle, Gutersloh, Paderborn, Detmold, Lemgo, Lage, Osnabruck, Herford, Bielefeld, Minden, Munster, Rinteln, Hohne, Fallingbostel, Soltau, Nienburg, Hameln, Wetter, Bracht, Hannover, Rheinzahlen, Hildesheim, Wolfenbuttel and of course Berlin. Some of these towns housed only a Regiment but several housed complete Brigades. In addition to the troops were their families and the schools, shops and medical facilities to support them all. All up total Brits, about 200000 (ish). Families had to give details of who could drive and were told where to go in case of evacuation (in the event that a war became likely). Those who could drive would drive other families toward the West.

The purpose of the forces facing the Warsaw Pact was to deter and, in the event that the Soviets crossed the Inner German Border (the fence) fight, delay and cause significant attrition, all to give time for diplomacy or the big red button to work. Life expectancy of an armoured soldier in combat was rumoured to be somewhere between three and twenty minutes.

It sounds like preparation for Armageddon. It was but some of the preparation could be fun.

Being based in Germany had a number of advantages over being based in the UK. One of these, surprisingly was that travel to the UK was not easy. Fewer people possessed cars than do today. There was no channel tunnel and flights were relatively expensive. These travel difficulties, combined with the fact that pay was not good meant that the majority of people, including single soldiers stayed within the Garrison. In addition, only 10% of any unit could be on leave at any one time, including over Christmas and the New Year so the forces were forced to make their own entertainment and to live cheek by jowl. It was, for most, a pleasant way of life. Anything was a good excuse for a party.

Accommodation, particularly for married personnel was much better than in the UK. Flats and houses were leased from the Federal German government. Mostly spacious and in a good state of repair it was accommodation that those in the UK could only dream of. They stayed in such good condition due to the efforts of military estate wardens who were stringent in ensuring almost impossibly high standards of cleanliness and serviceability were maintained. When a family was moving out of accommodation, spotless meant spotless and serviceable meant serviceable, or you paid regardless of the effects of normal wear and tear. Sometimes you just paid, because some of the estate wardens prided themselves on never having let a family away without paying for something....and yes, some of them really did use white gloves to find dust when inspecting a quarter that was supposedly ready for handover.

The majority of the barracks where single soldiers were accommodated survived from World War Two and had changed little since. Although generally better than accommodation in the

UK, conditions were spartan. The blocks were brightened up by the soldiers, but the main colour was a deep red due to the fact that almost all floors and window sills were painted with red oxide paint. Rooms were mostly 4 man rooms but some held 6 or 8 men. Each soldier moved metal or wooden wardrobes and metal lockers around to create at least some sort of private space. In married quarters you were given fairly modern beds (at least they had springs) tables, bedside cabinets, kitchen furniture, kitchen white goods and crockery and cutlery. As a living in soldier you got 3'x7' of space, a metal bed (which did not have springs but a web of V shaped metal attachments that supported the mattress), a wardrobe and a bedside cabinet. Wardrobes and bedside cabinets were often metal and a drab grey. As a result of these disparities between married personnel (pads) and single soldiers, "Pads" were reviled by the "singlies". Many years later as the first bases in Germany were closing down some soldiers were clearing a barracks and carrying the furniture down numerous stairs before throwing it all onto a large pile on open ground ready for destruction. The Staff Sergeant in charge of them (ex QOH) told them not to be stupid carrying it all downstairs but to throw it out of the windows and then sort it out once they had emptied the room or floor they were clearing. The Staff Sergeant then walked out of the building. Several stitches and a massive headache later he regretted the instructions he had just given!

Entertainment was varied. Married personnel could enjoy all the benefits of living in Germany which included an ability to travel within Germany, excellent but cheap food and an English supermarket (the NAAFI) in the Garrison. Single soldiers could of course enjoy the same benefits however the majority of single soldiers preferred to stay within walking distance of camp and entertainment revolved around alcohol, lots of it. Most units and sub units in any regiment or battalion had company or squadron bars. These made money for the unit and kept some of the single soldiers in barracks, so they did not cause a problem to the German population in the town. However, they also allowed soldiers to get tanked up with little or no supervision so that by midnight they were very drunk and wanting more so they headed for town.

As with most young people they needed something to rally around and as football clubs etc were not available they unsurprisingly supported their units. If anybody said or did anything against their unit fights would start. It was a nightly occurrence that for some became a culture. Local bars gained a reputation for being safe or not so safe. "The Ice bar" only had a few fights, "Potoffs" was a bar where anything went and if you wanted to guarantee a fight then the "Weinberg" was the place to go. The bars also became navigation points. Soldiers may not know this street or that street, but they did know "The Long bar", "The Kellar bar" or "Roxy's bar". Probably every soldier in Germany knew that Geordies Bar was on the main road through Sennelager.

Squadrons also had various squadron functions. The Squadron would hire a venue (using the funds it had generated in its bar) and all personnel would then go for a subsidised meal and a night of dance and revelry. Alcohol was of course consumed in large quantities and as there were no other soldiers to fight with, fights would sometimes start within the Squadron. Duty personnel had to be vigilant and often quite brave! Regimental functions ("all ranks" functions) were even more prone to punch ups due to the large numbers that attended (several hundred). Loyalty was first and foremost to those in your troop. If they got into a fight you helped them. Then it was your squadron or your regiment, in that order. If someone in your regiment was in a scrap you were expected to go and help him out. In addition there were Corporals Mess functions which Senior Non Commissioned Officers (SNCOs) and some Officers were sometimes invited to, Warrant Officers and Sergeants Mess functions during which some junior NCOs had to serve the food (not unpopular as it gave the opportunity to steal large amounts of drink and cigarettes) and Officers Mess functions which were often the most dangerous of them all due to the Officers habits of climbing buildings, shooting at each other with shotguns, tunnel rugby and numerous drinking games. For all of these functions and anything else that generated an excuse to drink, such as a sports match, the aim was to drink as much as possible. More senior personnel would tend to disappear relatively early during an evening to avoid any hassle. The day after functions the Regimental or relevant Squadron Sergeant Majors would then pick up the pieces and try to ensure that disciplinary measures deterred such behaviour in the future.

Sports were a large part of regimental life with footballers, boxers, skiers or rugby players becoming legend within their own units. They also managed to get lengthy periods of time away from barracks with skiers disappearing for months at a time and footballers and other sportsmen being excused all sorts of duties so that they could train every afternoon. Every Wednesday was a regimental sports afternoon. All were expected to take part in a sport (even angling counted). A few sneaked off to their rooms and a few more sneaked into town but they could expect no soft touch if they were caught.

Discipline was enforced in a number of ways. For some breaches of working practice, discipline on the vehicle park or whilst on exercise it was simply a case of inviting the guilty party to the rear of an armoured vehicle and then educating them by force. For those who think this harsh it was but when working with large and very dangerous lumps or armour discipline had to be good. There were of course those who abused their power and went too far becoming bullies and they were hated for it, but this practice stopped other forms of discipline which caused longer term pain being taken. Being charged usually resulted with a financial penalty or Restriction of Privileges (ROPs). ROPs were a particular pain as they meant you had not only to do additional work but also parade behind the guard showing various bits of kit in immaculate condition during the number of days you were given ROPs for. Extra duties were given for minor infringements or lots of extra duties for serious infringements. One particular Sergeant Major was often known to give 30 or more extra duties to an individual for a misdemeanour. One extra duty was a day and usually the night as well of additional and often unnecessary work. As Regimental Sergeant Major within the Warrant Officers and Sergeants Mess he would count three days (a weekend) as one duty.

One breach of conduct that was viewed very seriously was a single soldier making advances to a married woman. Sometimes they were successful. I lived in a quarter in a ten storey block of flats. Each flat had a small balcony (usually reserved for crates of beer or a fridge for the beer) and as I went onto the balcony on a very cold and snowy night I looked across at the opposite ten storey block. Suddenly a body leapt from a third floor balcony, a suicidal leap of about 40 feet. The guilty party landed in the snow, got to his feet and shuffled off in a run but with a severe limp. I knew the guilty party. When I asked him the next day what had happened he explained that the husband, who was on duty, had managed to get an hour off and had come home early. The only way of avoiding him was the suicidal leap I had witnessed. Given the size and brutal reputation of the husband (and for that matter the wife!) a bruised ankle was a good return for such a jump............if you will pardon the pun.

When based in Germany a regiment had almost all the equipment it would go to war with. A full complement of tanks, weapons and support vehicles. Each squadron had four troops each with three Chieftain and a Squadron Headquarters (SHQ) with two Chieftain. SHQ also had an AF 432 ambulance (that was almost always used illegally as a Command Vehicle), a Ferret Scout Car (Squadron Sergeant Majors vehicle) and a Land Rover for the Squadron Leader. There was also a contingent of Royal Electrical and Mechanical Engineers (REME) called the Light Aid Detachment (LAD) attached to the Regiment and split between the Squadrons. Each squadron LAD had two more variants of the AF 43 chassis, the AF 434 and AF 438 and also a Centurion recovery vehicle. All these vehicles had to be maintained so for the majority of the week the squadron worked on the "Tank Park". Chieftain was a tank soldiers tank. It could be stripped down to its basic components and put back together again by the crew. If there was something broken it could, sometimes with a lot of effort, be fixed. There was just so much that could go wrong. The engine was hugely underpowered for a beast weighing in excess of 50 tons but, as each crew had their own tank, pride was taken by most in keeping them on the road and in pristine condition. If one broke down and the spares were available, you worked on it until it was fixed regardless of the time of day or year. As is the case now, there were numerous inspections of the vehicle. Commanders functional checks, REME 857 inspections and the big one, the annual PRE (periodic REME inspection). The standard to achieve was to have no crew jobs outstanding and only three REME jobs. Any outstanding jobs had to be supported by evidence that a spare was being waited for and had been requested. Crews that failed to achieve this standard could be in for disciplinary action or at the least the Troop Sergeant got it in the ear from the Squadron Leader. Chieftain had a lot of oil in it. Gallons of oil for the generator engine, much more oil in the main engine. Thicker oil in the gearbox. The same thick oil in all the wheel hubs. Thinner oils in the various gun parts. Once something was broken Chieftain leaked. It still kept going as the crew would often just keep topping up with endless gallons of oil, the majority of which would be spewed out of the engine decks. The poor REME would then spend the night trying to fix all the tanks and then be expected to keep up with the Squadron, fixing vehicles as they went the next day. The ARV (Armoured Recovery vehicle based on a Centurion hull) was in constant use towing broken down Chieftains. The crew were generally kept very well supplied with beer as the usual charge for being recovered was a crate. When the beer extracted from the broken down crews ran out, the crew of the recovery vehicle, being REME personnel with initiative, often had a beer barrel and pumps rigged up on the back decks of the vehicle under a large canopy. This canopy was sometimes a disadvantage when trying to get into confined spaces in woodland or under a road bridge but as the vehicle became the hub of LAD activities and parties it was deemed worthwhile.

Tank crews lived on their vehicles when deployed on exercise. Everything that was done was done to a drill. Up and down drills were those activities conducted when getting the vehicle ready to go at the start of the day or parking up once the days activities were concluded. Up drills stated who would check the engines and tracks, cook breakfast, make sure the radios were working, take camouflage down etc. Down drills dictated who would cook, lay line (signals wire that was used in order to minimise radio traffic), put crew tents up, listen to the radios and go on guard. If there was unlikely to be time to erect tents a large waterproof sheet was placed over the back decks of the tank, supported by the gun barrel, under which the crew would sleep in their pre-designated positions. Tactics were all well rehearsed drills. Each commander knew what would happen when conducting obstacle crossings, planned attacks against enemy positions, withdrawal, advance and so on. The tactics were based in a large part on those used by the Wermacht during their withdrawal from Soviet forces.

To test a unit's readiness, the unit was "crashed out" of barracks to hiding areas at least twice a year (Exercise Active Edge). In eight hours all vehicles had to be deployed as well as a plethora of other stores and administrative "stuff". These crash outs were kept a tight secret and could come at any time, often when half the Regiment were in bars in the surrounding garrison and town. Had the Politzei ever breath tested a driver during a crash out there is a very good chance that the driver would have been well over the limit. Once the troops were in their allocated waiting areas (hides), an inspection team would descend and check guns and vehicle stowage. Stowage of tools and equipment had to be the same on all vehicles and a stowage diagram was held by all commanders. Even the bins had names. Drivers bin, gunners long bin, commanders bin (which had some of the drivers personal equipment in it) and so on. This ensured that any individual that had to move to another tank because theirs had broken/been blown up was able to find anything he needed to carry on the fight.

After several hours in the field during which time most had had time to sober up the crash out was completed and the Regiment returned to barracks, parked up the tanks and then returned machine guns and ranging guns and other stores to the Squadron Quarter Master Sergeant stores and armouries. Usually the whole process took the best part of a day. We could tell it would not be on a Tuesday as it would cock up the following days sporting fixtures but beyond that it was anybody's guess when one would occur.

Another element of the Regiment was Headquarter Squadron. This provided the logistic support to the Regiment but also the command elements and Reconnaissance and Guided Weapons troops. Reconnaissance troop was equipped with Scimitar (Ferret scout cars had been replaced in the mid 70's) and Guided Weapons troop (Gobbly Wobbly troop), which was equipped with another 432 variant, had Swingfire missiles. I don't know about Soviet forces, but Guided Weapons frightened the life out of me. On the rare occasion they were fired they seemed incapable of getting the missiles to go in the direction of the target. Often, they went in the completely opposite direction and headed back toward the launch vehicle!

Exercises were frequent. Between the towns of Soltau and Luneburg (the area in which Mongomery took the surrender of the Wermacht at the end World War Two) was the Soltau Luneburg Training area. Each regiment exercised here at least twice a year for two weeks at a time when they were not deployed elsewhere. There were the annual brigade or divisional exercises which lasted about a month and took place over the German country side. There were also a couple of bouts of range firing at Hohne ranges, each of two weeks. Visits to BATUS (British Army Training Unit Suffield) in Canada were frequent with two visits in a year not being unusual. Each visit lasted about six weeks. In total a considerable amount of time was spent out of barracks in learning the tank soldiers craft whilst living on the tanks. The Royal Armoured Corps was good at it, very good and we would have given a good account of ourselves had we been called upon to do so. We lived and breathed our tanks and we knew how to fight them. Years later a former East German officer who had remained in the German army after unification told me that Soviet pact forces were prepared to lose up to 13000 men per kilometre of advance. It brought into sharp focus why we needed to train so hard.

ARMAGH AND THE MURDER TRIANGLE – 1977

In 1977 The Queens Own Hussars were deployed on an operational tour to Armagh. The tour was a four month emergency tour from May to October. The Regiments Area of Responsibility (AOR) stretched from Cookstown in County Tyrone south to Armagh and its surrounding areas and covered the border between Aughnacloy and Keady. There were both Protestant and Catholic areas and it was certainly not an easy option for a Cavalry Regiment. Numerous attacks on both the regular Army and members of the Ulster Defence Regiment had taken place. Our main base was Drummad Barracks just outside the city of Armagh and we shared it with the Ulster Defence Regiment.

The Ulster Defence Regiment (UDR) was the largest Regiment in the British Army with 11 Battalions at one stage. Its soldiers were mostly part timers who lived amongst the community. As such they were easy targets for the provisional IRA and many were killed. Female members of the Regiment were known as Greenfinches. They also suffered heavy casualties. Although the UDR faced criticism throughout its existence for some sectarianism and other faults, those members that I met were both very brave and very professional.

At the time of our deployment I was a driver in Reconnaissance troop. The troops role as I saw it (a trooper's point of view) was to support the other squadrons in their areas of responsibility and to conduct surveillance tasks throughout the Regiments area. Our training consisted of fitness training, practising surveillance tasks and many, many hours of patrolling and conducting Vehicle Check points (VCPs). VCPs were set up using our vehicles to slow and control traffic that was trying to use a route by creating a chicane in which we could stop and check vehicles and their occupants. We also conducted "Eagle" VCPs. These were much more fun as we were taken on task in Scout or Wessex helicopters and dropped in a field close to a road in order to stop vehicles we had identified from the air. All great fun until the helicopter banked a little too steeply and one of the team fell out, held only by a canvas safety strap. It did its job and we managed to get the team member back in. If you want to watch 300 feet of pee falling away from someone....................that'll do it!

The majority of our training had taken place in Detmold where the Regiment was stationed at that time. One of the tasks we practised was the Observation Point (OP). It was not unusual for a team of four (known as the bric) to be in a location for several days so we practised moving in using dead ground and setting up an OP in a bush. One man would be on guard, one would be watching the target and two would be resting. That was the theory. Before we went out our kit was checked to ensure we had what would be needed and once deployed in the field we practised ration drops and getting rid of our waste. This would take two men with all the waste (including human waste) leaving the OP and going to a prearranged point to hand over the waste and collect the next couple of days food. It was hardly a balanced diet consisting mainly of cooked steaks and cold Steak and Kidney pies, but it was filling.

When deployed on practise OP's we learned useful lessons. I learned that it was perhaps not good to drink all your water on day one and then fill your bottle up from a ditch that ran next to the OP. When my stomach began to complain and I realised my bowels and I were about to part company I asked my compatriot to pass me a plastic bag out of my large pack which he duly did not do. He saw my discomfort smiled and delayed handing the bag over. Eventually after what seemed an age (but was in reality only a second or so) he handed it over but it was too late! Plastic bags when pulled tightly do not go into nice tubular shapes that fit bottoms and I missed the bag, promptly filling my sleeping bag hood with what can only be described as a brown liquid! Great.

I cleaned the sleeping bag as best I could with grass but then it started to rain. Sleeping bags at this time had a waterproof side and a non-waterproof side. To keep dry you simply turned the waterproof side up and slept in the bag. The next two days were possibly the least fun I have ever had. Warm, wet and very, very smelly.

13

Our final training was conducted in a purpose built mock up known as Tin City in Sennelager. Much of it was constructed of corrugated iron, hence the name. We were accommodated in a tented camp called Woodlands and bussed from place to place for various training serials. On arrival at Woodlands we were informed that paper was precious so if we needed to go to the toilet we could have three sheets," One up, one down and one polisher!" Trunkie Howard, the Quarter Master at the time, was not smiling when he said it. I used exactly three sheets on each occasion I visited the toilet for the next two weeks.

On one training serial we had to go through a CQBR (Close Quarter Battle Range) where we would use blue plastic bullets in our rifles (the 7.62mm Self Loading Rifle). These could, if they hit you, leave a nasty welt and there was more than one fight as a result of a miss aimed shot.

Our team commander had seen the CQBR in action and had taken note of one of the traps laid for the unwary. He warned us all not to take cover by the petrol pumps as "the enemy" were ranged in on it. When it came to our brics turn, we left the waiting area and the petrol pumps were in front of us. We began to "hard target" and our bric commander immediately took cover by the petrol pump. He heard a noise and looking up he got smacked straight on the bridge of the nose by a coke can full of soil! Lots of blood! Great fun taking the piss. Just brilliant. He took it all very well, but it must have really hurt and he looked bruised and battered for quite a while after we completed Tin City.

Once we arrived in Northern Ireland, at a time when the Improvised Explosive Device had claimed a lot of lives we travelled to Armagh from Belfast by bus. What a target. A sigh of relief on arrival and we were taken to our rooms. Drumadd Barracks was pretty new in comparison to our accommodation in Germany. The vast majority of rooms were for four men, ideal for accommodating teams. The washrooms were modern and clean and in general it was the best accommodation I had yet been in, including my time as a Junior Soldier in Bovington. There was a helipad near the accommodation which doubled up as an excellent volleyball court although you had to be quick moving nets when there were incoming flights. The barracks was about 700m in length with towers (sangers) surrounding it in which I spent many hours on guard.

Armagh is not a large city. With a population at the time of only 14000 or so it was the fourth smallest city in the UK, however it did have staunchly Catholic areas where republicanism was rife and the provisional IRA (PIRA) could operate with some support. The Culdee and Drumagh estates were estates where you watched your surroundings very carefully. The ability to move quietly at night was removed by the amount of broken glass strewn in every alleyway. Dogs were definitely not friendly and the residents were, on occasion, surly. The Culdee estate was fairly close to the city centre and the Drumagh estate was a little further west, about 500 metres apart at their nearest point. Despite these enclaves the city was relatively quiet and the Regiment suffered nowhere near the hassle troops were receiving in Londonderry and West Belfast. Trouble in our area was mainly in the rural areas.

To combat the movement of weapons and men we were constantly busy conducting Vehicle Check Points and patrols all across the regimental area. Despite the threat of Improvised Explosive Devices (IED), movement in vehicles was still the norm. Our main modes of transport were the Saracen (a six wheeled armoured car with a turret that carried a GPMG or .30 machine gun) or the Land Rover. Neither was exactly covert. The Saracen was huge and you can hear a Land Rover travelling at any speed over ten miles an hour from a long distance away. However, they were a lot more comfortable than foot patrols.

Armagh is blessed with some very big hedges. Many of them are blackthorn hedges with vicious thorns that easily penetrated clothing and occasionally boots. You could not use gateways and obvious gaps (what are now called Vulnerable Points) due to the threat of IEDs so you were left with climbing barbed wire fences or climbing through blackthorn hedges whilst on foot patrols. Patrols of both sorts were on average about eight hours in length. In some area's the patrols could be broken up by a tea stop. In Protestant areas much of the population wanted nothing to do with any form of trouble including that wrought by Protestant para militaries. They bravely invited us into their homes and gave us tea and cakes. One of these stops was a couple called Ma and Jack. They were a wonderful kind, elderly couple and almost all patrols that went through the area in which they lived used to stop at their house. It must have become very obvious and rumour has it that on one occasion after our tour a pressure plate was discovered close to where vehicles would park when patrols stopped. Twenty one years later I would go on foot patrol in County Armagh again. There were still Blackthorn hedges and there were still Tea stops. Mobile patrols were restricted to certain safe areas due to the ongoing and constantly evolving threat from IEDs. The majority of movement was by helicopter.

As Recce troop we conducted a number of OPs, some of them lengthy ones. The first OP we conducted was a classic example of how not to do it. Two teams moved into a barn and almost immediately were discovered by the farmer (looked a little terrified with a rifle placed under his chin). An A Squadron troop leader then proceeded to reassure us that the farmer had sworn to secrecy, so we could go ahead and occupy the OP. Oh really?! That OP did not last long.

On another occasion, we were given the task of watching a point where a farm track crossed the border. We moved in well, occupied the OP and settled into routine. I am not sure exactly how long we were in place for, but I spent my rest hours writing ridiculously long letters to my then girlfriend. They must have been very much like facebook now. Updated every few minutes and very, very boring! I wrote several letters over a hundred pages and the team went through the resupply routine at least twice, so I think we must have been in place for about a week. Nothing, except for a very pretty young woman who was caught short and used the large pillar of a gate by the border as cover. A significant amount of money in terms of observation equipment was deployed in her direction at that particular moment.

It was whilst returning from one of these OPs that my first and only contact during that tour occurred. We had been picked up by one of our mobile patrols in Land Rovers. As they were fully crewed for their patrol we squeezed our two teams in with theirs. As we travelled through a mainly protestant area one of my team shouted, "Contact!" (The term used when "Contact" with the enemy was made). We then went into a complete buggers muddle of a contact drill. The first man to exit the rear of my land rover almost bit the carrying handle off his Light Machine Gun as he caught the muzzle on one side of the rear door and the butt on the other. Blood before we had even started.

Both the teams that had come to collect us were commanded by Corporals. Our two teams were commanded by Corporals. A number of different words of command were being issued at once. "Take cover!" "Follow me!" "Open fire!" Three corporals, three simultaneous words of command. The fourth just looked puzzled and wondered what all the fuss was about. Eventually it all calmed down. No one opened fire. I had taken the "Take Cover" word of command as the most sensible and fitted neatly into a ditch about six inches deep at the side of the road. Two other members of the troop had wormed there way up to where the shot or shots may have come from and found nothing, so we waited for the Cavalry. This arrived remarkably quickly in the form of B Squadron Leader, Major JJ Phipps and his Land Rover group. He took one look at the situation, told us to get on with it and dismissed it as a non-event. He was a vastly experienced soldier but even after all this time I am not convinced that a hostile shot was not fired at us. I subsequently found out that the dog that was brought in as part of the follow up found an air scent (a scent laid in the previous fifteen minutes) of a human in the area we suspected was the firing point and then followed that to a recently burnt out vehicle. Strikes me as being suspicious! As it was we got a lot of flak and the micky taken out of us severely.

Our saddest day in province was the day after a failed OP. We had been operating in the Stewartstown area. Stewartstown was to the West of Lough Neagh in County Tyrone between Cookstown and Dungannon and was a republican area. We had been tasked to mount an OP on a pub in the town, but the only viewpoint was a building about eighty yards from the pub and the only access was a set of external steps. We had a UDR Lieutenant with us that night who could identify the target we were supposed to observe.

After hours of preparation and rehearsal we made our approach and were on the steps when Murphy's law kicked in and someone came out of the pub and saw us. There was nothing we could do but cancel the OP and carry on as if we were on a normal patrol. When we returned to Drummadd barracks the UDR Lieutenant had given us a few bottles of beer which we accepted with glee. The next morning, he was ambushed by the IRA and killed as he went to work. Over the next couple of nights, we patrolled the area he had been killed in. When one of the patrols was finished and we were cleaning up one of the lads bragged about stealing a white towel off a washing line. He was using it to dry his face. He could not understand the laughter until he took a closer look and saw that the towel was a nappy and had not been washed that well!

Night patrols in rural areas were often hard work, particularly for the man carrying the radio. The "portable" radio in use at the time was the A41. This was a heavy beast with heavy batteries and was clamped onto a heavy metal frame. It weighed a lot. During a night patrol on a beautifully moonlit night we had to cross a ditch that was about 7 feet deep and about as wide. You could clear it with a running start and a good jump. Three of the four of us cleared it. Then it was the radio operators turn. You could not see him clearly but you could hear the thump of his feet on soil then...."Ughh" as he failed to make the jump and his midriff hit the opposite lip of the ditch then, "Bollocks! Twat!" as he slid down into the bottom of the ditch, followed by a splash and several giggle filled minutes as we tried to retrieve him and the radio.

We operated out of the Royal Ulster Constabulary (RUC) station at Stewartstown on several occasions. On one of these I was on guard and manning the gate letting vehicles in and out. This had to be done quickly as the one entrance to the RUC station was a vulnerable point and could easily be targeted. As an RUC armoured Land Rover went to leave I ran to open the gate. I opened one gate and then moved to open the other.

Why is it that when someone has hurt you (other than deliberately) they always ask, "Are you all right?" This is what the RUC officer was asking me as I realised I was lying beside the gate with my beret in the gutter and my rifle in the road. Being run over hurts! In the RUC haste to leave they had gone for it with only one gate open and had hit me in between gates. I have been run over twice in my life. Both times by Land Rovers in Northern Ireland!

Recce Troop 1977

Front Row L-R: Cpl Dave Shiers, Cpl Freddie Cairns, Cpl Taff Bullock, Capt M Bromley-Gardner, Sgt Bob Biddle, Cpl Phil Green, LCpl Paul Booker.

Middle Row L-R: Tpr Steve Plumridge, LCpl Peabody, Tpr Steve Meads, Tpr John Cook, LCpl Clive Greig, Tpr Bayliss, Tpr Steve Green, Tpr Vic Daborn, Cfn Geordie ?.

Back Row L-R: Tpr Brian Sumner, Tpr Shell Merriman, Tpr Herbie Kings, Tpr Tom Hamilton, Tpr Sean McLean, Tpr Chris Gould, Cfn ??, Tpr Mick Broom.

8ᵗʰ HUSSARS, HOHNE

Just before amalgamation (4ᵗʰ and 8ᵗʰ Hussars) with a visit due from Prince Philip, the 8ᵗʰ Hussars CO, Lt Col Pat DeClermont decided that all officers should be mounted for the parade. On the first rehearsal the Regiment formed up in squadrons with all officers duly mounted with sabres drawn. Truly a magnificent sight. That was until the first order, "Royal Salute" was given. With the first beat of the bass drum and the Band at full blast the parade turned into chaos. Just like a Western Rodeo horses turned into bucking broncos, out of control and the troopers running for safety. Col Pats' charger took off to the next barracks. We in the band were having a great laugh making as much noise as possible. We reformed about 20 mins later and minus lots of horses, we eventually produced an excellent parade for His Royal Highness.

Baz King Regimental Band

IRISH/BRUMMIE UNDERSTANDING

As the QM, my remit during pre Northern Ireland training was to visit all the locations the squadrons were using on Salisbury Plain to carry out rural training, prior to deployment on an OP BANNER tour in 1998. I remember pulling in to see the SQMS of C Squadron and found him in a foul mood. I would point out at this juncture that he was an Irishman with a very strong Northern Irish accent, that in truth you had to be attuned to. He offered me a cuppa and we then discussed his reason for being in said mood. "I sent Tpr Smith out for a Six Foot table about an hour ago and when he gets back he is going to get both barrels as the table is just at the back of this building!". Strange thought I, as Tpr Smith was not the sharpest tool in the box but he certainly wasn't daft. Anyway, I didn't give it another thought and discussed the issues of the day with the SQMS and enjoyed the tea. I left his office and got back into the MK2 Combat Camper and my driver proceeded to the main gate. As we went around the corner of the building I spied Tpr Smith looking around the perimeter of the Camp. We stopped and I called him over and asked what he was doing. 'Looking for Sixty foot of cable Sir' – Bless him. Chuckling, I pointed out that it was a six foot table he was meant to be looking for, and that it was behind the outside door to the SQMS's Store.

Paul Hodgson

WARNING – GUARD DOGS.

An Irish Battalion occupied a barracks in Munster. The RSM had been told that as guard dogs were now being used to patrol the perimeter the perimeter fence had to be marked with the correct signs. Calling in his Provost Sergeant he briefed him on the requirement of the signs and then walked the perimeter fence with the Sergeant to see how many signs were needed. Having completed the walk he told the Provost Sergeant to get a sign made up so that he could check it before the remaining signs were made.

The Provost Sergeant decided that the RSM did not need to be disturbed to check on such a simple task and after a few days he turned up at the RSMs office.

"Right Sir" he said in a broad southern Irish accent. "The signs are up. All done."

The RSM reminded the Sergeant that he had wanted to check them but thanked him anyway and then carried on with his days work. Just as he was preparing to go back to his quarter the Commanding Officer phoned him and suggested he might want to check the perimeter fence. A feeling of dread came over him. The signs were up, every fifty yards as discussed. Yellow as discussed. Each gave a warning and showed the head of an Alsation in silhouette, as discussed.

"Warning – Guard dogs on petrol!" NOT as discussed.

ANDERSONSTOWN 1979

In 1979 The Queens Own Hussars deployed on a six month tour to Andersonstown in West Belfast.

'A' Squadron were deployed to Woodburn (not far from the Twinbrooks estate), B Squadron and the Close Observation Platoon (provided by the 16/5th Lancers) were in Glassmullen, in the centre of Andersonstown and C Squadron and RHQ were in Fort Monagh, along with The Kings Own Scottish Borderers, beside Turf Lodge.

Training for the tour had been similar to that undertaken for the emergency tour to Armagh in 1977. Endless practice patrols and lots of vehicle check points. There was an increased emphasis on searching buildings and much more emphasis on urban patrolling. Tin City (a purpose built urban area in Sennelager, Germany) was the culmination of training. Each team and group of teams (a multiple) was put through its paces practising all aspects of patrolling, cordons, riot drills and what to do in the event of a shooting or bombing. The civilian population (Civpol) for Tin City was now provided by another regiment and riot training, in particular the phase in which you move in to grab a particular rioter (use of a snatch squad) was very realistic. There were a number of injuries as each side of the riot (civpol and the Regiment) tried to outdo each other in realism. The flak jackets we wore were good enough to stop a brick breaking a bone and perhaps a low velocity bullet at extreme range but they were extremely warm. When you got back into "Fort George" (the notional security base) after a training serial there was always a big sigh of relief whilst you shucked off your flak jacket. This respite lasted until your drills were ripped to pieces during a CCTV debrief by the training teams. The system of training at Tin City had matured a lot in two years. There is no doubt in my mind that the training saved lives, both civilian and military.

As we did on any deployment out of Germany to Canada or Northern Ireland, we flew out of RAF Gutersloh, about a 45 minute drive from Hobart Barracks in Detmold. RAF Gutersloh was huge and could easily take large aircraft. The flight to Aldergrove took about an hour and a half however the whole business of moving took 24 hours. The RAF movers had (and still have) a system known as MCCP or Movement Control Check Point which happens in barracks. 24 hours before the flight we were all checked through the MCCP then the whole process was repeated about 8 hours before the flight. Then we were moved to the airport where "Crab air" movers would go through the process one more time. The arrival process at RAF Aldergrove in Ireland was much quicker and it was only an hour or so before we were in coaches with a large armed escort on our way to our various locations in the West of Belfast. As a member of B Squadron I was on my way to Glassmullen. I was shattered when I arrived as at 0600 on the morning I deployed I had been on Commanding Officers Orders for being involved in a fracas with members of the Royal Welsh Fusiliers. This was slightly annoying as we had meant to get revenge on a group of Blues and Royals (now part of the Household Cavalry Regiment) for beating up one of our soldiers and had not expected a large group of Welsh Fusiliers in Detmold. They were based in Lemgo, about 10 miles away. The Welsh Fusiliers, unfortunately, "got it" by mistake! I was remanded until the end of the tour and was pretty sure I would lose my Lance Corporal stripe.

Glassmullen camp was situated on Slieveban Drive in the centre of Andersonstown. It was also known as silver city as its perimeter was comprised of corrugated iron walls about 20 feet high with sangers on every corner. The whole camp was only about 200m long and 100m or so wide. Accommodation was in single story prefabricated huts which could house about 30 men and had basic toilet and washing facilities. In a few areas bullet holes showed on the tin walls. I do not recall much concrete protection and a mortar attack would have been devastating. As I recall, there was no such thing as Hesco (metal cages filled with stone and used as protection) in those days. There were some low brick walls between living accommodation blocks but that was about it.

Our regular tasks consisted of urban patrols, escorts (providing escorts for supply runs or personnel movement) and guard duties which were split between guarding Glassmullen camp, Musgrave Park Hospital and supporting the Royal Ulster Constabulary by guarding the police station on the junction of the Falls, Glen and Andersonstown roads, RUC Andersonstown. Patrols were clearly the favourite activity because guard duties are guard duties wherever you are.

One drawback with patrolling was having to clean flak jackets on our return from any urban patrol. This was not due to any of our activities but due to the habit of the local youths in spitting as much phlegm as they could over our backs. Usually it was young girls. Another habit of the locals was to train their dogs to go for anything in uniform. It was hard to concentrate on watching your arcs on a patrol when there was a dog snapping at your ankles trying to eat bits of you. On one occasion, an instructor from the Northern Ireland Training and Advisory Team (NITAT – the organisation that trained all troops for NI deployments) came on a patrol with us. As we arrived in the Rosnareens, (an area close to the Glen Road) a pack of dogs began to harry us. The instructor worked from the script and told us to ignore the dogs and watch our arcs. About twenty seconds later there was an agonised cry of, "Aaagh you fucker!" and he was minus about a pound of calf muscle. He had to be evacuated by an RUC mobile patrol with blood pouring from his leg. Needless to say, we ignored the NITAT instructors advice and kept a very close eye on the local dogs.

Although dogs caused problems they occasionally ended up on the receiving end. There was one particularly large dog (nicknamed Gums) that specialised in chasing Land Rover patrols. No one was very bothered by this mutt, despite its size. It chased us in silence. It had a silent bark and no teeth as a result of a rifle butt being thrust down its throat when it tried to attack a patrol at some time in the distant past. It was sad that an animal had suffered but also amusing that it could look so menacing as it chased us in a gummy silence.

On another patrol, a member of one of our teams fired a shot accidentally. Other patrols in the area correctly reported a "contact" and began to hard target. The patrol that had initiated the incident, being unsure of exactly what had happened also reported a contact and went into a hot pursuit with some members of the team being convinced the shot had come from a nearby building. One large member of the team involved, seeing the door to the building was shut decided a shoulder charge would open it. He hit the door hard, it gave a bit, bent a bit, gave a bit more and then catapulted him backwards, straight through a greenhouse which then slowly collapsed around him. All this action had taken a matter of seconds. By the time the patrol member had picked himself up and dusted himself down it was clear the cause of the shot had been a negligent discharge and the patrol commander was trying to let everyone know that there was no need for the Commanding Officers Rover group, nor half of the West Belfast Police force, nor the helicopter, nor the hundred and one other agencies that would begin to spring into action when a contact (an engagement involving weapons) was reported.

During another contact a gunman fired several rounds at one of the B Squadron land rovers. Four or five rounds entered through the front window of the vehicle, passed between the commander and driver and travelled out through the rear of the Land Rover. The rear man in the vehicle looked down to see that at least one of the rounds had passed through the flies of his lightweight trousers and had come very close to preventing him from ever fathering children.

Riots were a regular event in West Belfast. It did not take much to give the youth of the city an excuse to gather and throw rocks and petrol bombs at the security services. The Provisional IRA sometimes used these gatherings as a shield for a shoot, weapon movement or as a "come on" to draw security force personnel into an area they had placed explosives. One particular day a prominent nationalist was addressing the crowd at Roger Casement Park in the centre of Andersonstown. As this was a scheduled event there had been significant planning of what to do in the event of trouble and my troop was "In reserve". Other troops were placed along the anticipated route of those leaving the stadium. As we were in reserve and not expected to get involved in any riot we only had short (four foot) riot shields and a few baton rounds (a baton round was a large cylindrical chunk of hard plastic designed to inflict a nasty bruise on a rioter as an alternative to lethal action. The round was fired from a baton gun and one was supposed to bounce them off the ground so they hit rioters at about waist height.)

As the speaker finished the youths began to pour out of the park and to look for trouble. Their aim was to prevent the security forces seeing where the nationalist speaker went. The crowd headed up the Andersonstown Road, passed the Kennedy Way roundabout and toward the RUC station. A large section of the crowd managed to bypass the waiting troops and get into the back roads between the Falls and Glen Roads. The reserve was quickly deployed to prevent a large scale incident at the RUC station. As a member of the reserve I and seven others with two Humber Pigs (the armoured box like vehicles in use in the city) found ourselves face to face with the crowd. There was a short lull and then the rocks came in. The locals quickly saw we only had short shields. If we lifted them to protect our heads they went for our legs and as we dropped then to protect our legs they went for our heads. The only way of keeping them back was with the baton guns. In no time we had used the few rounds we had and had to request more from the RUC station. These duly arrived and we kept firing as quickly as we could. I clearly remember one individual using a dustbin lid as a shield. I fired at the road and the round skipped up hitting the edge of the lid and smacking it into his face. Lots of blood. I turned with a huge smile to look at the team members behind me and saw with horror the worlds press. No more smiling! Bad PR! Eventually other teams arrived and the crowd broke up having achieved their aim as far as I could tell. I think I and the other baton gunner in my team fired some forty to fifty baton rounds during the incident.

During a disturbance in the west of Andersonstown there were two incidents of note that I remember. We were conducting a planned arrest (lift) of a known nationalist. As such there was plenty of support and several armoured vehicles were present. The size of the security presence led to a rapid response from the local youths and bottles and rocks were soon incoming. One bright spark threw a bottle at a "Pig". The bottle flew over the pig and hit another rioter on the other side of the road, knocking him senseless. The "Paddies" had a very efficient casualty evacuation system and he was soon dragged away. Someone in that same "Pig" then saw a rioter kneeling behind it. Two baton guns poked through the slit aperture in the rear doors of the Pig, slowly pointed almost vertically downward and fired simultaneously. The casualty evacuation teams were needed again.

The final riot "funny" took place on the Suffolk Road. This was the border between the A and B Squadron areas of operation. Much of the road has high embankments on either side. Some members of the Regiment already knew it well due to riots they had policed in an earlier tour in 1974. As we drove north on it toward the Glen Road we saw a man trying to remove a small tree that had been dragged across the road. There were several reasons that tree was there and none of them were good. Looking at the top of the bank we could see a large group of youths running to intercept us. It was clear we were going to be ambushed with a barrage of bricks. In an open topped Land Rover this was not a good experience. We went for it. Over the log as fast as we could. Large bump, look behind us. Lots of disappointed kids and a man jumping up and down with his hand to his mouth where he had clearly still had it under the small tree as we had gone speeding over it.

I have said that much of the tour was fun. It was but there was also a deadly serious side to it. People died during our tour. I mentioned earlier a shoot that had taken place. One of the Provisional IRA suspects was captured but later released. His body was found on the border with the Republic later that day as someone thought he had passed on information. In another incident a young man who was joyriding was shot and killed by members of another regiment after his car hit a member of one of their patrols. The soldiers opened fire hitting the man in the shoulder. The Self Loading Rifle was a powerful beast, far more so than its replacement, the SA80 and it practically ripped the young man's arm off. The bullet had ricocheted off a bone in his shoulder and the girl passenger with him was wounded by the same round.

On 27th August there were two major incidents that occurred in other parts of Ireland. A well planned attack at Warren Point near Newry saw the death of 18 members of the Parachute Regiment and in another attack Lord Mountbatten, along with members of his family, was murdered in the Republic. One of our patrol tasks on that day was to try and gauge public opinion and to ask locals we stopped what their views were. There was clearly satisfaction at the death of the para's, hardly surprising as we were in staunchly republican West Belfast but there was muted sympathy for the Royal Family over the death of Lord Mountbatten.

Eventually the tour came to an end. The 4/7th Dragoon Guards took over from us and we headed back to Germany and the Cold War.

Posing before deploying on civil disturbance duties. "Ox Haines" and Paddy Moore in the background. Note the length of the Self Loading Rifle (SLR), not brilliant in an urban environment.

CHURCH PARADE AND THE CHARGE OF THE LIGHT BRIGADE

Baz King, Band.

Colonel J. T. Paley, MC

Col John Paley had the nickname "Capbadge" Paley due to the fact he carried a buttonbrush in case he caught anyone with a dirty badge. My favourite recollection of J.P.is when the Regiment were marching to church in Hohne. Guidon flying and Major J.P. leading with sabre drawn, we passed two young German soldiers who failed to salute our Guidon. J.P. brought the parade to a halt and sabre waving rushed at the pair and gave them an almighty bollocking in fluent German. He then sent them 50 yards further on where they gave a smart salute as we passed. I bet the pair thought their time had come. Another memory was when we in the Band played at the Odeon Leicester Square at the World Premier of the film "Charge of the Light Brigade" Always a military perfectionist he was so annoyed that all the Troopers in the film wore 11H cherry coloured overalls that he left the cinema. No doubt he gave his views to the film makers. What a man, a true legend.

SOLTAU

The Soltau Luneburg Training area was situated between the towns of Soltau and Luneburg on the north west German Heide (Heathland). The main training area was approximately 24 kilometres long by 14 kilometres wide. A further area (the extension) of approximately fifteen by twelve kilometres was reserved for light armoured vehicles. There were normally two armoured combined arms groups training throughout the year, close to 200 armoured vehicles and a thousand soldiers at any one time. For most of the week you could train anywhere on the main area but at weekends you were restricted to smaller areas known as the Red areas (simply because they were red on the map). Originally known as Whisky, Victor, X Ray and so on, they were later numbered.

All armoured soldiers spent a considerable amount of time on Soltau, usually two exercises each year, sometimes three in years that part or all of the Regiment was to go to BATUS (British Army Training Unit Suffield) in Canada. Conditions were atrocious in both winter and summer. When it was wet the whole area turned into a sea of mud, particularly the red areas that had been stripped of any vegetation by years of churning tank tracks. When it was dry those areas that had been liquid mud turned into clouds of dust that attached itself to any moist area of the body and made all those on the area look as if they were coal miners wearing dark mascara. The dust was comprised of very fine grains that hung in the air for an age and made the act of travelling in a column of tanks an unpleasant (and very dangerous) experience for all but the lead tank. When it snowed which it inevitably did during winter, the pine trees held great mounds of snow that would fall as the tanks went close by, often engulfing a turret and catching those with open hatches unaware.

By far the worst conditions were when it was wet. It is a miserable existence inside a turret when it is raining. Rain drips through the hatches, seeps through almost all the sight housings and makes the interior of the turret filthy. Kit left in baskets (including large packs and bergens) was soaked and, worst of all, so were the camouflage nets. These nets were approximately six metres by six metres or bigger and were made of a network of thick string with large patches of uneven, torn green material attached to them. A tank has a myriad of sharp corners, nuts, bolts, wipers and worst of all, antennae bases with wingnuts. An individual has buttons on pockets, pens, a nose. "Cam nets" would catch on all of them, seemingly at once and when they were wet they soaked everything they touched. Common practice was to take the cam net off the vehicle, lay it out and then erect a sort of garage for the tank to drive into. Once on the ground it would pick up every branch and twig it could, doubling in weight. String or more often signals cable (D10) was tied to the corners of the cam net and then to spanners or heavy tools. These were then thrown over branches. What goes up must come down and often there were sworn reproaches as another crew member got a spanner to the head! The net was then hauled into position, the tank was reversed under it and the remaining camouflage drills then conducted, including covering the tracks the tank had made. Camming up when it was wet was a lengthy and soul destroying task. Camming down, the reverse process was equally fraught. Each stick had to be picked from the nets which were then folded in the right way so that they fitted into their stowage position without obscuring the vision through any of the sights.

To the north of the training area was a nature reserve. Very, VERY out of bounds but inevitably the odd lost vehicle would crash through the fence and enter it. There was no hiding the damage the tracks of armoured vehicles could do on the sandy soil, nor the miles of crushed saplings that resulted from the excursion and bollockings would then flow down the chain of command to the hapless commander. One Royal Tank Regiment commander must have spent several hours on the nature reserve judging by the motorways he is reputed to have carved.

There were two constants about Soltau. Dirt which got into everything from clothing to oils, and "Wolfgang". Wolfgang was a local German entrepreneur who, knowing that Brits had a liking for chips and Bratwursts bought a van, converted it into a mobile chip shop and then drove around the area until he found the soldiers.

After a little while he got to know exactly where soldiers would be and at what time. It was rumoured that he had radios in the back of the van as well as maps of every exercise ever conducted but in reality it was just his experience of the almost constant presence of troops on the training area. Wolfgang could drive off the road and into a wood where there were no visible signs of any soldiers or vehicles. He would then ring a very loud bell attached to his vehicle and troops would appear from every direction, racing to be first in the queue so they got their food before being told to get back into the woods as they were supposed to be training!

Despite the rough terrain and the fact that often only tanks seemed to be able to move Wolfgang would arrive with his van. He rarely got "Bogged" (stuck in the mud) but on those rare occasions that he did it was not long before a tracked vehicle had towed him out (free chips) and he had made his way off to another company or squadron position.

Although the training area was fairly large the fact that it usually had a minimum of 150 armoured vehicles and 800 to 1000 soldiers on it at any one time meant that movement and training had to be strictly controlled. As various different elements of a training package were completed squadrons and companies moved from one red area to another for the next element of training. Each red area suited a different type of training aim. Area 1 (W and V) was good for advancing. Area 2 (X ray 1 and 2) was good for practicing assaulting fixed positions and for obstacle crossings. Movement was often at night, cross country and tactical which meant no lights. Commanders and drivers became adept at night driving. Commanders would not look at the ground but look up and follow the gaps left in the tree canopy by the track they were following. Drivers could either risk driving closed down and use their image intensification sights (first generation and about as much use as a chocolate fireguard) or drive opened up and concentrate on "feeling" the ground as they got to it. This was a difficult skill made all the harder by the fact that they were trying to keep up with and follow a very small light on the rear of the tank in front. This light would go up and down with the tank and at least gave a clue if they hit a big hole. In dusty conditions this "convoy" light was not visible. Moving at night in a column was very dangerous indeed and on several occasions there were nasty accidents, some of which resulted in fatalities. Commanders had no GPS and younger commanders frequently got lost (more experienced commanders generally had a good idea of where they were as they had been on the training area so many times). Inevitably the lead commander was the youngest troop leader or the troop corporal. Those following would then engage their thumbs in their rears and put their brains in neutral and just follow without paying any attention at all to where they were. Most were inside their turrets having a cup of tea or a beer. If the lead vehicle got lost, then they all got lost. On one night move a young troop leader decided he would lead. After becoming lost on several occasions and being corrected by the troop sergeant and troop corporal he lost his temper. At that time the tanks were equipped with Larkspur radios that had large hand held microphones with a rubber mouth piece. The annoyed troop leader smashed his microphone down onto the armoured hood of his commanders sight. The microphone did not break but bounced and hit the troop leader in the head. He collapsed back into the turret, unconscious. After a brief talk with his crew to assess that he was still alive the troop corporal took the lead and the troop made its way to its night time location without further mishap.

Night moves were also a hazard for the local population. Some of the routes taken by the tanks crossed public roads and on more than one occasion a civilian car had ploughed into the side of a tank whose commander, not knowing quite where he was, had failed to turn his lights on at the junction. In the winter, mud left by the tanks was a danger as it turned the roads into an ice rink. Despite the hazards the locals were surprisingly tolerant and polite.

One really dangerous track ran down the side of one of the red areas until it came to a junction with several roads (known as Picadilly junction). In winter it was mud six feet deep and sometimes even the tanks could not move on it and in summer it became gritty and dusty with no visibility at all. There were fatal accidents on this track due to its nature and the conditions under which soldiers had to use it. I once watched a REME soldier having to completely submerge himself into the deep mud in order to fit a tow rope to a bogged tank.

One very unpleasant hazard of Soltau was as a result of the numbers of soldiers that used it. Up until the 1990's portaloos were not used and soldiers would wander off into the woods for a "shovel recce". That is a lot of fertiliser on a daily basis! Crews spent much time in creating their own comfortable loo's. Usually the loo was a 20 litre oil can with its top cut off and masking tape wrapped around the edge to provide a comfortable seat. This was then tied to the back of the tank where it was promptly covered in oil. Comfortable maybe, clean and hygienic it was not.

Whilst preparing to give a camouflage demonstration to his squadron, one commander was camouflaging his tank. The camouflage nets had been hung and he was now laying turfs over the front of the vehicle and the turret. He had cut several turfs when his gunner gave a gleeful shout. "Look! There's some ready cut turfs here!" The experienced commander knew what was under the ready cut turfs but did not have time (nor the inclination) to yell a warning. The next sound was of the gunner swearing and wretching as he realised the soft mud under the turf that he had scooped up was not mud.

Once training for the day was finished the tanks would usually pull in under some trees, "Cam up" and wait for the next activity. This was usually a "Replen" where the Squadron Quarter Master Sergeant (SQMS) would bring up the logistic support required to top up the vehicles for the next day. The bulk of this support was fuel. In the days before fuel bowsers all fuel was delivered in Jerry cans (a 20 litre can, invented by the Germans during WW2). A tanks average for a days activities was about twenty cans which had to be collected from the fuel vehicle (unless it was able to squeeze between the trees and pass the cans straight onto the back decks of the receiving vehicle), carried to the tank, emptied into the fuel tanks, thrown off the tanks and then carried back to the fuel lorry. Trying to refuel quietly was impossible. You could hear a troop refuelling from a hundred yards away. Eventually some bright spark invented the fuel bowser but the fuel bowsers engine was also very noisy. Sleep was a commodity hard to come by. The other type of "replen" was the "rolling replen" where the tanks would drive alongside various supply vehicles picking up what was needed. Usually this was fuel (the empty cans were thrown off at the end of the replen for the SQMS to collect) and at least an equal number of "Yellow Bricks" of Heforder pils (6 bottles to one yellow box). If the night was tactical (guards out, no lights or noise and an early move) crews would traverse the gun to the rear, stick a large rubber sheet used to cover the turret during moves by transporter known as the tank sheet over the back decks supported by the gun and sleep on the back decks. Usually the driver or commander closest to the rear of the vehicle and the two of the other crew members nearer the turret. The fourth crew member would be on guard or listening to the radios and the crew would hot bed during the night. On nights where there was no tactical training there was an opportunity to let your hair down and have more than a few beers. On more organised "Squadron smoker" nights the whole squadron would gather round an enormous fire for a barbeque and a drink. Much of the training areas woodland must have disappeared over the years. The sound of an axe was common. When the next days activities began crews were often still very much under the weather.

After two weeks the exercise was normally finished but it was often not the end of the deployment. The tanks would regularly move straight from the training area to the Bergen Hohne tank ranges, travelling some 30 Km down a route known as the Weitzendorf corridor, that bypassed the town of Soltau and the major roads. A measure of the success of this route march was how many tanks actually arrived on the ranges. Usually it took at least a day to patch up, repair and recover those tanks that had broken down on the route.

As a result of the demise of the Soviet Union, Soltau was eventually closed down in 1994. (Perhaps we should now open it again!) Given the number of tanks that had used the area, all of them leaking oil to some extent or another it is a miracle that the greens and those seeking compensation for the environmental damage done found none. The training area is now a beautiful area of heathland visited by tourists and locals.

DRIVING INSTRUCTION.

I was an operator in Recce troop parked in strip wood on area 2 (X ray for the older and bolder than I) watching an A Squadron troop moving up the side of the training area. One thing about Soltau was it was a bitch to drive over as the ground was like a roller coaster after years of armoured manoeuvre. One tank in particular seemed to have an inexperienced driver as you could plainly see the commander being thrown about in the turret each time the tank hit the bottom of a rut. It was probably made worse by the fact the gun was rear so the commander could not sit down if he wanted to see where he was going. There is a way to deal with rolling ground, dropping revs just as the tank begins to dip forward and then revving up as the tank begins to climb the far side of the rut. Suddenly the tank stopped. The rest of the troop were still moving so I presumed it had broken down. Not uncommon. The driver clambered out of his cab and then stood on the glassis plate so that he was level with the commander. As the drivers head appeared above the level of the turret the commander threw a right hander. The driver flew off the tank in a star shape and landed in the dust in front of the tank. He then climbed back into the drivers seat and moved off much more slowly. That is what you call driving instruction.

WIVES CLUB VISIT.

On occasion the wives would be driven from the home base to visit their husbands on the Soltau training area. Those that wanted to could have a drive of an armoured vehicle (NOT allowed today) or clamber all over one, or they could wander off into the surrounding area to chat with hubby about kids and things. One wife who had wandered off with her husband came back with him just in time for the BBQ the Squadron was having to celebrate the wives visit. Before the visit, the husband had been working on his vehicle repairing an engine fault. That had left oil over his hands which had neatly transferred to her white top, leaving two perfect handprints across her chest. Neither had noticed on the way back to the BBQ. It was only when several of the lads volunteered to see if their hands would fit the outline that she became aware. Two colours then featured. A very red blush and then the air turned blue as she turned to her husband.

THE D10 MOMENTS.

It was quite common for the tanks to lose internal communications (IC) between the crews. This could be pretty dangerous if the driver could not hear the commander. One ruse was to put the gun rear and use the signals wire all the tanks carried (D10) and tie it to the epaulettes of the driver. The commander could then pull on his left shoulder for "Go left", right shoulder for "Go right" and pull both at once for "Stop". When it worked it allowed basic movement. When it went wrong it caused panic. Commanders could be seen climbing on moving tanks trying to stop their drivers before carnage ensued. Several damaged tanks and other vehicles are a result of moving with no IC.

F COMPANY

Soltau training area was often used for pre BATUS training. On one occasion we had spent a very wet and miserable two weeks training with F Company of 1 Scots Guards who would be our infantry support in Canada. The Brigade Commander decided he wished to address the Battle Group and the only place to do that was in the middle of area 2. The RSM gave instructions to form a hollow square. 'A' Squadron fell in, 'B' Squadron fell in, 'HQ' Squadron ambled up. Three sides of the square complete. The fourth side was formed by a huge puddle about a hundred metres long. Where were F Company? "Duff, Dite, Duff, Dite.........
Company........alt!" The company marched up as if on Horse Guards and halted in a line that followed the edge of the puddle. The Company Sergeant Major (CSM) leant forward and cast a critical eye down the line. "Right Turn!" He cried. Like clockwork the company turned in unison but still no feet were in the puddle and there was a big bow in the line. The CSM, no neck and a solid

38

Glaswegian accent picked on the smallest lad (in the centre of the line as he should be). "You! Get in the puddle!" There was no movement, just a look that said "Really?" from the comparatively diminutive guardsman (You had to be over six foot something to be in F Company!). The CSM gave him a withering look and then in a voice that brooked no argument, "Ay! You! Get in the fuckin' puddle! Now!" On the final "Now!" the guardsman jumped forward both feet together and landed about three feet into the lake. The CSM looked, then looked again then staring at his company as if wishing someone to argue shouted, "Cover off!" The company moved as one. Big splash. Straight line. CSM smiled then turned with an immaculate drill movement in the mud and reported the Company present and correct to the RSM. That BATUS was one of the best I had seen and the guards were fantastic.

The only blip on that pre BATUS was that RHQ invited the CO and RSM of 1 Scots Guards for dinner in the field. As usual 0H (zero hotel) was deployed. This was the Officers Mess four ton truck which had tent, tables, cookers, washroom, kitchen sink et al. Dinner was served with full silver, waiter service and music. The visiting RSM said that we should not have gone to the trouble of laying all this on. Being ex SAS and a died in the wool carry a knife between your teeth sort of bloke he was shocked when he was told this was how RHQ always dined by a pissed RHQ troop Sergeant who benefitted from the same service (until he got his mess bill). It was only when tactical that the Officers would get their food from the back of a darkened 0H and forego the silver service.

PUFFING BILLY

One item of equipment that no good headquarters in the field would be without was a "Puffing Billy". This looked like a dustbin with a chimney and had a petrol burner in it. When lit it warmed up water so that the officers had warm water for a morning wash. The poor unfortunate who had to light the puffing billy (either the last man on guard or a mess steward that had been dragged out on exercise solely to make life comfortable for RHQ officers) was at considerable risk. The technique was to fill a tray with petrol, throw a match down the chimney and hopefully the burner would light. It was an endless source of fun to listen to the whoomph of the billy being lit and then the, "Shit that hurt!" pause, whoomph! "Bollocks!" pause, whoomph! "Aaaargh!" Eventually there would be a whoomph followed by, "Thank fuck for that!"

You could usually tell who had got the task of lighting the puffing billy. They had no eyebrows!

SINGLE LIFE IN HOHNE: 1985-1992

Andrew Milton

As a result of still being in service at the time of writing, some of the content to follow has been edited (or perhaps should have been omitted.)

Having spent over 18 months as a "singlie" in West Berlin, moving to Caen Barracks in Hohne Camp was a daunting prospect and many of the single Berlin lads were adamant that they were signing off.

Berlin had been a single soldiers dream posting with all ranks having their own room and amazing nightlife. The Squadron (Sqn) consisted of many characters, some of whom it was clear you had to show respect to and be careful how you spoke to them. The Berlin Sqn consisted of the more experienced members of the Regiment with a close to operational role as we were surrounded by the Warsaw Pact and quite often under the watchful eye of the Russians. The rest of the Regiment was back in Catterick as the Training Regiment, so it was quite an honour to be part of the fighting sqn. I had actually been sent to Berlin from Catterick as a punishment as in Captain Mellor's words "I had got into the wrong crowd". The single days in Catterick are a chapter on their own!

Before moving to Hohne the Berlin Squadron was shipped back to Catterick for the Tercentenary Parade. I was in quite a predicament as the night before we had taken some of the 14th /20th Hussars over to the East to show them the sights, which meant wearing NO2 dress, which officially you had to change back out of before socialising in the West. On the way back, I decided I wanted to show them one of my local haunts, "Mon Cheries" which was in the red light district. The show consisted of different acts culminating in two of the customers being taken into a big bubble bath with the ladies. I had tried my hardest to be selected, however for some reason the lady I had been trying to impress decided to choose an elderly man next to me and took great pleasure in making me feel rejected! Enough was enough. I put my red hat on, saluted and dived into the bath causing the ladies to flee. They even closed the bath lid on me. The threats of being handed to the Polizei were enough for me to leave. The next morning things were not so amusing. My No2 dress was soaking and the Maid of Warsaw Badge had turned pink! I had no choice but to bundle them wet into a bag and put the bag in my case for the journey back to UK.

We were taken to Rotterdam to catch the overnight crossing to Hull. The crossing was certainly eventful, as there happened to be a party of Dutch college girls en route to UK to play in a netball competition. They became quite attracted to our "Cool Dudes" and were soon on the dance floor with them. The College leaders were not impressed and rounded them up to send them to their cabins. They ended up patrolling the cabin corridors to keep our blokes away and looked shattered the next morning at breakfast. We also had an incident where Michael "Honey Monster" Pinch and Steve "Scottie" Scott were caught by the Ship's fun police running around with sheets over their heads, running into cabins acting as ghosts. In the end the Captain made the decision to invite us all down to the crew bar to keep us out of mischief and away from mere mortals.

We eventually arrived at Catterick where I instantly ran down to the Dry Cleaners to get my No2 Dress sorted. The lady working there commented that they were only fit for the rag bin but in the end she did a sterling job and other than being a bit tight I was able to go on parade in them. The Commanding Officer, Lt Col Jenkins on his inspection actually commented on how smart I looked!

Shortly after the parade we arrived at Hohne, which was around the corner from Belsen Concentration Camp. The camp had been used as an SS barracks during the Second World War and after the liberation of the concentration camp it provided temporary accommodation for those who had managed to survive. Other than internal improvements to the accommodation little had changed and it was very easy to imagine how it must have been for the Third Reich soldiers during those years, especially when visiting places like the main NAAFI (Navy Army and Air Force Institute), called the Round House. This had been used by the SS for grand social events, the fittings and ornaments were intact.

The tank ranges nearby meant we could stay in our own accommodation during live firing periods which was an advantage in some ways but a disadvantage when other units were using the ranges, especially during night firing when the rattling of windows would wake you up .

Nightlife when compared to Berlin was dire. The Garrison consisted of about 3,000 troops, including us, Welsh Guards, 2 Artillery Units, all the other supporting arms and a Dutch tank battalion, who all had to frequent the small town of Bergen. There were three main bars and a nightclub called Mic Macs, which was the battle ground for inter regimental brawls. Some of the Welsh Guards were complete thugs who took great pleasure in beating up naïve newcomers who ventured out to experience the German night life. It put me off the Welsh for a very long time, until I met my current girlfriend who lives in Pontypool. I can even manage a bit of the language, but this is not public knowledge!

It soon became apparent that in order to reduce the injuries down town our squadron bars needed to be the social hub, a place where even the married people (pads) could come and socialise.

I started my Hohne days in B Squadron under the excellent management skills of Major Timmy (Squeaky) Watts (Squadron Leader), Captain Billy Budd (2IC) and WO2 Frank Chambers (SSM). Serving during their tenure were probably my happiest years of single life. B Squadron really was a fun and happy squadron and a lot of this stemmed around life in the Squadron bar. It really was a hive of activity.

The bar was built by Martin Skipp who managed to get all the old fittings from a German bar, which had been renovated. The only thing missing was a decent bell, so I was given the task of acquiring one. It was during this period that the IRA had been active against troops in Germany so security on camps was at it tightest. This didn't' stop me and the gang getting under the wire of Brigade HQ and taking a lovely brass bell that we had spotted while on guard there a few nights previously. We had a dry run whilst on that duty and loosened the fittings ready for the taking. I am led to believe the bell is still proudly on display in B Squadron bar.

Billy Budd was having great pleasure in inviting local brewery representatives to come along with samples in the hope we would sell their beer. One particular afternoon we had a very generous brewery rep and Billy was a bit the worse for wear. He lived on camp and was trying to cycle home but could not get peddling. I noticed the child seat on the back of his bike and managed to persuade him to sit in it while I cycled him home. We had to go down the main road to get to his married quarter and it certainly was a sight, a Captain in uniform sat in the kid's seat and we were all over the place. I tried to avoid going past the RMP duty room, but he insisted we did. I tried finally to ride in a straight line without looking in and noticed Billy had thrown up a full salute. We managed to make it to his quarter and just as Jan his wife came running out to complain about Billy being an embarrassment, we fell off the bike.

The first beer to be introduced was called Lindener which was a strong local beer and one we could not handle. At times it resulted in the bar getting trashed much to the annoyance of Martin Skipp. Despite changing the strengths of beer to conserve the bar there were still occasions when the décor suffered, I can remember being barman and Paul "Mamf" Manfred and Dave "Tommo" Thompson were on vodka frenzy, every time they finished they threw the glass on the floor toasting Brezhnev. Somehow this turned into a tomato ketchup battle, followed by me spraying them with a large foam fire extinguisher. The next morning the bar looked like a winter wonderland massacre.

There are numerous tales about the Squadron bar which could be a book on its own, however I will record a few tales, some where people will remain nameless and others where I've toned down the content in order not to jeopardise anyone's reputation. It was not just the Singlies who frequented the bar, especially on a Friday afternoon when after the Colonel's run there was always a "Happy Hour" where much troop business was done. Quite often wives would turn up late in the evening to drag their husbands out. Our Squadron parties were always well attended and rarely without an incident, often involving the married people. One married bloke was caught by his wife with a blow up doll (which had been a farewell present to Dave "Logie" Logan) in the Squadron Orderly Corporal's bunk. On another occasion we ended up with guests in the bar who were visiting Hohne, one of whom was a lady with a wooden leg. She soon became quite drunk and ended up on the dance floor to the lively music the bar was accustomed to. I'm not sure how it happened but somehow, she fell over and her wooden leg had fallen off. This would have been an ideal souvenir for many of the singlies but decency prevailed and after some slight embarrassment she was reunited with it.

The Squadron Orderly Corporal (SOC) had his duty room opposite the bar and for the married JNCOs (Junior Non-Commissioned Officers) it was a duty they never complained about. They took great pleasure in participating in the Squadron bar drinking games such as shock dice and spoof. The bar stayed open until last man standing, which was often the SOC shortly before going over to the accommodation to do reveille. Although there were official closing hours, rarely were they adhered to, even when the Orderly Sergeant and Orderly Officer appeared. It would not take much to persuade them to join in and on one particular occasion a new young Officer (who will remain nameless) came off slightly the worse for wear. We had just arrived back from Canada all very jet lagged and decided the only way to recover would be to have a few beers to help us sleep. The young Subaltern realised he was on a lost cause trying to close the bar so decided to participate in the drinking. He had recently arrived so had not been in Canada and soon grew tired of hearing all the tales, making it quite clear that we were boring him. His comments became quite offensive and I could tell that he was on borrowed time before he was dealt with. I decided to call the Duty Driver and informed the young Officer that it was time for him to go before someone "filled him in". At the top of his voice he told me where to go in no uncertain terms which resulted in a queue of blokes wanting to sort him out. Tommo and I managed to drag him out of the bar before there were blows when half way down the stairs he clenched onto the bannister and would not let go. Tommo had a particular party trick called "Master Blasting" which consisted of holding his foreskin tight while building up a pressure of liquid. He would then press the bulge, which resulted in the liquid coming out like a fire hose. He decided that "Master Blasting" the young Subaltern was the only way to persuade him to let go of the bannister. Give the Subaltern his due, he decided to retaliate in the same way but did not quite have the same size equipment as Tommo. Once we got him to the Duty Driver's Land Rover he would not get in and was insisting on having a helicopter. It was obvious he was totally pissed so we sent the Land Rover round the block and on its return pretended it was a helicopter by doing landing drills. We soon had him strapped in and off they went to Schloss Bredebeck (The Officer's Chateau). We all returned to the bar thinking that the Officer had got away relatively unscathed. This was not the case. It turned out that when they got close to Bredebeck he decided he wanted to parachute in and before the driver could do anything he dived out through the door. The next morning he certainly looked a sad state not to mention what the state his NO1 Dress (Blues) must have been. He insisted he could not remember anything and to this day I am really not sure if he could.

Tommo's "Master Blasting" was one of many of his drinking antics. He was always regarded as the innocent one if ever there was any trouble. On one particular occasion, when he had vandalised the bar, Frank Chambers was blaming me and even when Tommo went to own up, Frank would not believe him and told him to stop covering for me. His luck finally ran out when, during a Squadron fancy dress party, he drove out of camp to pick up one of the pads and was stopped by the RMP (Royal Military Police). He got out of his car dressed as a baby, with nappy, bib and dummy in his mouth but the RMP did not see the funny side.

The Squadron barman was a voluntary duty, normally for a month and when doing this you did not have to work on the Tank Park. Despite the stock checks, it was a good money maker as you could do your own food and there were many scams. I did it on many occasions and despite my awful music such as the "rodeo song" and "Brother Louis" I always had a well attended bar. On one occasion Americans troops were over from the States on Exercise "Reforger". They were in the transit accommodation and were not allowed out of camp. I soon had them all using my bar. They only had dollars and did not seem to complain about my excessive exchange rate. By the time they left they had presented me with a medal for allied relationships and a lovely girlfriend called Laura. She really was my proper first love and within no time she had managed to get a posting back from the States to Germany, so we could be together. Unfortunately, her camp was 4 hours south in Hanau and despite the weekend visits things became difficult, especially when it transpired she had moved over with marriage (!) on her agenda. We had a big fall out after drinking one afternoon on a bank holiday Sunday. I ended up getting in my VW Beetle and tried to drive back. Luckily my guardian angel made me see sense and I pulled into a lay by and slept it off. I was woken the next morning by loud horns from several trucks as I was blocking the exit onto the Autobahn. I returned to Hohne and wallowed for a few weeks until my old mate Stephan "Zac The Lad" Zacwych persuaded me to join him on a holiday to Thailand for 3 weeks to cheer up. I managed to pay for this out of all the profits I had made from running the Squadron bar. Tommo joined us and those 3 weeks in Thailand soon confirmed that I was not ready for marriage.

The Regimental restaurant was commonly known as the "Cook House." The food and accommodation charges were very reasonable and were deducted from your wages at source. I am now witnessing a "pay as you dine" system which has ruined the perks we could get with the old system. I will always remember John Hosey, the Master Chef who struck a deal with me when he caught me filling a fire bucket with food to take back to the Friday afternoon "Happy Hour" in the bar. The agreement was that I would give him numbers of those who wanted to stay in the bar and he would put the right amount of food into a tray for me to take over. Once the cookhouse was closed, he would then come to the bar and would be rewarded with free drinks.

The military chefs cooked quality food and were always flexible with the work pattern on the Tank Park. We were able to book late meals if working late or quite often they would make up "wraps" (takeaway) for us to take back to those still working.

The only down side to our cookhouse was we shared it with the RMP living in members who at times took a bit of stick especially if we had come over from the bar. We were marked men and quite often those of us who were fortunate to have cars were pulled over and given all the checks they could do. They got their revenge one day when the Duty Driver from HQ Squadron came in to the Cook House after a squadron party the night before. Someone shouted over to him about his antics that previous night and this was noted by a table of RMPs and resulted in an RMP breathalysing him on his return back to the Guard Room in the Duty Land Rover. He was over the limit and his career suffered accordingly.

On another occasion a group of us were walking down the road after a particularly social afternoon in the bar when an RMP car slowed down and started following us, much to our annoyance. I decided to give them monkey impressions, which they did not take too kindly to, resulting in them pursuing us. I managed to get away but tripped over, grazing my face from forehead to chin and smashing my new watch, which had been a birthday present from my parents. Andy "Burnie" Burnett came off even worse. They grabbed hold of him and Burnie being Burnie thumped one of them. He was bundled into the car, taken to our guardroom and placed in close arrest. We went over to reason with Dave "Lips" Lewis who was the Orderly Sergeant and while we distracted him Burnie escaped. He did not go very far, straight to the NAAFI bar where he was promptly rearrested by Lips.

I always feared Monday mornings. If I was not in front of the SSM pleading my innocence, I was outside the RSM's Office. This particular Monday morning we were lucky. Jimmy Baker, C Sqn SSM was standing in for the RSM who was away. My face was a right mess and once he heard the full story he was quite sympathetic, however it did not stop Burnie having to do some time in the cells once the RMP reports were processed.

I had quite a few run ins with the RMP, some funny trivial incidents and others more severe which I won't repeat until I've finished my service. One worthy of mention was the robbing of a Christmas tree for the accommodation, I was with a young Jamie

"Boo" Fright. It was planted in a German's garden and we had not noticed them watching us as we pulled it out of the ground. As we were walking back to camp with it on our shoulders I noticed an RMP car approaching so we quickly threw it to the side and carried on walking. The RMP car passed us but quickly turned around when they saw the tree by the side of the road and they arrested us. Boo was new to the Regiment, so I told him to deny everything as we had not actually been caught with it. We were taken to the Guard Room, separated in different cells and given the "nice guy, bad guy" treatment. Boo's "nice guy" RMP interrupted my "bad guy" interview to explain I had better go and chat to Boo. He had fallen for the "no charges will be pressed if you admit to it" routine. Boo tried to convince me that all we had to do was take the tree back and apologise to the owners. A few weeks later it was CO's orders and a £100 fine.

For years I tried to avoid contact with RMPs and have a quieter existence. After my service with the Regular Army I managed to get a full time SQMS contract with 37 Signal Regiment, a reserve regiment in Redditch. I was very lucky to get the job however my line manager is an RMP! My SQMS dodgy dealing has had to stop. I still find it a struggle to accept the RMP way of working.

The RMP were not the only ones we had incidents with. The local Provost Sergeant was a rough character who you avoided, in the name of Sergeant Ginge Ingham. Rarely did you get the better of Ginge. I did on one occasion when he was driving slowly up the back road to camp looking for someone to shout at. I overtook in my car wearing an old man mask and making gestures to him. This resulted in a car chase round the whole camp. He never caught me on that occasion but the next time he saw me I was soon wearing a steel helmet because apparently my beret was wrongly shaped. I decided to shine the helmet till it was silver in colour and stuck a cap badge on and wore it down to the Round House. Ginge had no choice but to take it back off me!

Despite living close to the RMPs our accommodation was of a high standard in comparison to some camps in Germany. Each troop had its own flat complete with kitchen, TV room and fully fitted rooms, which were single for NCO's and 2 man rooms for troopers. On arrival at Hohne before the Berlin Squadron was disbanded I shared a room with Howard "Pig" Robinson. He certainly lived up to his name, but we got on so well I ended up as his best man. Little did I know that 15 years later I would be with him when he died in hospital from cancer. A legend it has to be said!

My B Squadron single life as a trooper was spent sharing a room with Simon "Sam" Davies followed by Clem Wallace after Sam got married. I was lucky that neither of them snored and we shared similar interests, women and booze! Our troop decided to buy a communal tropical fish aquarium. It was placed in the TV room and to start with it was our pride and joy, but the novelty soon wore off. Every morning we would discover dead fish and the water looking a rather strange colour. In the end we were left with just a big Crayfish, so we decided to sell everything to Yvonne who worked in the cookhouse. She did not want the crayfish so sadly it was lobbed out of the window and was later found dead but quite a distance from our block. It had nearly made it to water!

Along with Clem and Sam, B Squadron singlies consisted of many social animals. Dave "Tommo" Thompson, Simon "Spunky Spaniel" Hartnell, Jamie "Boo" Fright and Dave "Logie" Logan to name but a few. There were many living in characters and one in particular was Lewie Wright. He had worked in the stables for years but been sent to us for allegedly poisoning one of the horses!! He became the SQMS storeman, which was certainly a challenge for the SQMS, Taff Cattell. I had a love hate relationship with Lewie and have to admit I certainly wound him up on several occasions. My room was directly above his and I would dangle a spoon on some string out of the window and keep tapping it on his window below, but at a distance where he would have to lean out to grab it. Poor Lewie would fall for it every time, as soon as he leant out of the window I would tip a bucket of water over him!! There were many antics I played on Lewie. One in particular was when they promoted him during his last year in service. I had been bust back to trooper and happened to be on guard with Paul "Rodders" Greves when Lewie was Squadron Orderly Corporal and I found him asleep in the Bunk. I decided to wake him up by shouting his name whilst pointing my Sub Machine Gun (SMG) in his face. He flipped and got a penknife out and started chasing me. I was halfway down the stairs and thought I could defend myself by hitting him on the legs with the SMG as he came down. I whacked him several times, but he did not flinch. Next thing I knew he cut my hand with the knife. I had to go to the hospital (MRS) and have stitches!! I was soon back on duty to discover Lewie had woken properly and written the whole scenario in the occurrence book. The pages were numbered so we had to rewrite the event to minimise the outcome for both of us.

It was a sad day when it was time for Lewie to leave the Regiment. Most of those he had joined up with were now Warrant Officers and we held a small party in HQ Squadron bar to say farewell. I was particularly honoured that he invited me, so I brought him a present. He not only thanked me for the present but informed me, "you kept me bloody young by chasing you round camp". Shortly after he left we were given some terrible news, poor Lewie had been knocked down and killed by a bus. By the time we received the news his funeral had taken place. I'm sure there would have been a regimental turnout to say farewell if we had known. RIP Lewie.

Sometimes some of us would go and see the sights. The red light districts of Germany were not seedy in any way and were regularly visited, particularly the Reeperbahn in Hamburg. This was only an hour up the road from Hohne and most singlies will have Reeperbahn tales to tell. Zac "The Lad" worked in the PRI (regimental shop) and one of his duties was driving the regimental coach, which often did trips back to UK. If he was not driving to UK he would organise trips up to the Reeperbahn more for his benefit than anyone else's, particularly with the fees he charged!! It was not only at weekends we would venture up. I remember one night I was moping in the Squadron bar as I'd been stood up by the Colonel's nanny who I had met earlier in the afternoon. It was late in the evening and Sean Ryan decided to cheer me up by organising a trip up to the Reeperbahn that night. We got back just in time for work.

The chances of getting a German girlfriend were very remote due to the ratio of soldiers to local Bergen girls and those who were successful had often had to lower their standards. It was not unusual to see a familiar girl in the block with a different bloke. Simon "Spunky Spaniel" did manage to find one who started coming back to his room on a regular basis, however for some reason she took a dislike to me. This soon came to a head when one evening I bumped into her in Mic Macs and my one liners resulted in her head butting me. I knew my revenge would come and that evening she returned to the block with Simon. I decided the fire hose needed testing and along with my trusty pal Clem I tested it in on her in Simon's room. She was not impressed and swearing in her broken English told me she intended to run me over when she next saw me in her car. It just so happened she had driven into camp that night, so to prevent this I decided to let her tyres down. The next morning, she stormed into my room threatening to call the Polizei. Her English translation of what had happened to her car was so comical I agreed to sort it out. She was never seen in the block again.

I did manage to find a local German girlfriend for a while, Suzie. She was a true example of the "Master Race". Blond hair, blue eyes and a personality to go with it. She was also quite well known amongst the Garrison and had a young black son who slept in her bedroom. She shared the small flat with a friend we nicknamed the "Bull Frog".

Whenever I met up with Suzie, the "Bull frog" would come along and I would have to get her fixed up to be allowed to come back to the flat. I would take them up to the Squadron bar and ply someone with beers, a tactic my mates were accustomed to and despite their initial refusals it normally worked. It would be quite comical seeing them the next morning at the flat!! I can recall a commotion one night when Zac had fallen for my tactics. We were woken by a bang and lots of shouting and went rushing into the room to discover Zac had got up and banged his head, cutting it on the unit above the bed. It was not a pretty sight seeing a naked "Bull Frog" dabbing his head with a tissue with a naked Zac shouting all sorts of expletives.

I'm not sure how it finished with Suzie. It was either when I took her on a tour with a visiting civilian rugby club to the Reeperbahn and there was a punch up, or my antics at a rugby third half. Although not quite the correct build to play for the regimental rugby team I went everywhere with them including a tour back to UK in the capacity of Sponge Boy/Song Master. If we were winning by a large margin I would have a quick go on the wing but normally my duties consisted of running on with a sponge I had specially purchased, a big pink heart, which the players tried their hardest to avoid. Our results as a rugby team were not the best but I made sure we never lost a third half. Over the years I had managed to memorise various rude songs and drinking games, which got the respect from the opposing team. The third half antics were hilarious and involved games such as bombers (where you carried as many 10p coins as possible in the cheeks of your bottom and accurately deposited them in a glass) and boat races (drink a pint of anything as quickly as possible) with lots of drinking and unruly behaviour, however there was never any trouble or anyone requiring a stomach pump. I think it was me drinking a pint of "anything" that eventually changed her mind about me.

Push bikes were always sought after especially when out socialising. I and Tommo had an unfortunate incident when we robbed a bike from outside one of the blocks to go and visit my old troop Sergeant from the Junior Leaders Regiment. He was with 1 Royal Tank Regiment and they were staying in the transit camp. We found him in their bar and I was trying to convince him that I had grown up and was taking my career seriously when the QOH Orderly Sergeant, Pete Lund, stormed in out of breath and fuming and telling us to get to jail. It was his bike we had nicked and somehow he had managed to track us down.

The journey back to camp from a night out was always quite adventurous and if we weren't stealing bikes we were souvenir hunting from the transit accommodation next to us. There were often different nations units staying, displaying attractive flags or signs, which invariably ended up in our TV room. On one return journey, we went to the NAAFI for a late night pie and found one of the confectionary machines insecure. In no time the boxes of Mars Bars and Wispas etc stored at the bottom were over in B Squadron accommodation for late night "munchies". We were woken next morning by the SOC informing us that the RMP were about to search the block as one of the NAAFI machines had allegedly been broken into. The SOC was Dave (Geordie) Byrne and it soon became apparent to him by all the sweet wrappers who the offenders were. He managed to stall the RMP while we concealed the evidence in the woods behind the accommodation. We also decided to hide all our souvenirs from the TV room and it was quite a sight, seeing us all running out with bikes and signs etc. The next day we went to recover everything. The bikes and signs were OK but many of the chocolate bars had animal teeth marks in them. We still ate them!!

Life as a singlie certainly had its advantages over the Pads (married blokes) apart from if somebody hadn't turned up for Guard Mount (normally a Pad). The Orderly Sergeant would come straight to the singlie's accommodation to find a replacement. First parade was at 0825, where as long as you were on parade the troop Sergeant turned a blind eye to how intoxicated you were and he turned another blind eye if you went into the driver's cab of a tank to recover. The excuse was checking the driver's batteries and you would then get woken up at 1000 by the clunking of the bollards (large metal tow hooks on the front of the tank) to go to for a half hour morning break at either the NAAFI or their mobile wagon. Lunch was from 1230 -1400. In the early days at Hohne the NAAFI bar would be open for the "hair of the dog" and for the Pads to have a beer. This changed as we tried to lose the BAOR (British Army of The Rhine) "drinkers" image. More often than not, lunch break was a time for recovering from the night before. Generally, we finished work at 1630 however we did have a readiness role to meet the advancing Russians if they had decided to cross the border. If a new engine or gearbox turned up, we worked until the tank was ready to roll again. Once again, we would rely on the cookhouse to give us a carry out (wraps) rather than stopping work to go and get cleaned up for evening meal. They would always do enough to cater for the pads too.

Our state of readiness was often tested by a crash out known as Exercise "Active Edge". We normally had an inkling it was going to happen, but we were never confined to camp so the RMPs would go around the bars in town announcing it had been called. They would then see us a few hours later in tanks trundling through their control points with the drivers who had been in the bars earlier. It was often quite a drive to the locations where we would set up a defensive position ready to meet the advancing enemy. Apparently, our life expectancy as a front line tank crew was 20 mins.

Being a front line armoured regiment meant we always had to have a certain percentage of crewmen back in Germany so leave had to be staggered. The Regiment had block leave periods and would leave a rear party to do the duties. I l always volunteered to do rear party as the duties only came round every few days so there was lots of time off and when the main party returned you then went on leave so in effect you had a month off the tank park. Quite often I did the bar for the rear party and on one occasion Captain Reg Taylor, the Sqn 2IC asked me to look after his son's Goldfish as he and his family were going back to UK. The afternoon before going on leave he brought the fish bowl up to the bar during a happy hour. There were two Goldfish and he explained that one of them was not very lively and may not survive. The bar was quite busy and Corporal "Jabba" Hutt from the REME decided he wanted to eat the fish which was not in the best of health. He would not shut up about this damn fish, so I placed the bowl in front of him and true to his word he put the fish out of its misery. He then became even more annoying boasting about the REME and their antics and challenged someone from QOH to do the same. I took up the challenge. We then had an empty fish bowl! As Reg was not going back to UK until the following day I became slightly concerned that he may come to the bar later for a visit, so I sent someone down to the pet shop in Bergen to buy two replacement fish. He came back with a bag of six, so we had to get rid of four by having a QOH versus REME fish-eating contest. By the next morning I still had an empty fish bowl!! Goldfish had become a Camp delicacy.

The day before everyone came back off leave I went and purchased two fish just in time before Reg came up with his son to collect the fish. He seemed very surprised that both had survived but I could tell his son was not convinced. Years later the truth finally came out at one of my Worcester troop reunions, with Reg finding it all very amusing.

Priority for Christmas and New Year leave was always given to the singlies but once again a rear party was always required. If you happened to be one of those on rear party you would be woken up on Christmas morning by the Squadron Leader, SSM and SQMS with a concoction known as "gun fire". The taste would change every year depending on who mixed it and which spirits needed shifting from the Squadron bar. The hierarchy always ensured we had a pad's house to go to for Christmas dinner, where we were always well looked after, even if they did have to draw straws to take some of us. During the summer months we were quite often invited to BBQs and in some cases, we took it upon ourselves to call round and insist on one. I remember we bumped into the SQMS, Taff Cattell and his wife "Sid" in The Roundhouse and informed them we would be calling round. We caught up with them an hour later pushing a trolley full of beer back to their married quarter.

QOH really was a family regiment with many social functions and activities. The All Ranks Functions were particularly good fun and rarely did they pass without an incident. There were quite often inter squadron games and competitions. I believe I am still the reigning regimental disco dancing champion, after an event where the smoothies in the Regiment tried to impress the ladies with their moves. I got up after a few beers too many to compete and the wives who were the judges took sympathy and gave me the title.

Squadrons took it in turns to organise the All Ranks Functions which was always an onerous task, particularly when trying to get everyone out at the end of the night. I was certainly one of the offenders to the detriment of A Sqn SSM, John Nason, who had organised one with his Squadron. He asked me to leave and did not get the answer he wanted. Woody from the REME was walking past with a complete leftover gateaux and John told him to put it in my face. Before he had chance, I bet Woody to do it to John instead, I could not believe it he actually did! John was covered but still took it as a joke. I'm not sure if SSMs nowadays would react in the same way but I still see John at reunions and memories like this give you something to talk about.

The Garrison bonfire night was a commitment B Squadron picked up one year. The Brigade Commander was to light it, so our LAD of the REME tried to make their name by rigging up a detonator linked to trip flares with a handle for him to push. Things did not go according to plan and the Brigadier could be seen pushing it several times without anything happening. Eventually one of the LAD went and pulled the wire linked to the flares but for some reason only one went off and the fire just started smouldering. In no time the whole crowd was engulfed in a big cloud of smoke. The LAD never lived it down and we never let them start our Exercise Smokers after that. There were many characters in the REME and like all attached "Cap Badged" soldiers we treated them as our own and sometimes they would transfer in.

One particular bonfire night everyone came back to the bar loaded with fireworks some of which were pyrotechnics which had not been handed in after an Exercise. The majority of the fireworks/pyrotechnics were fired out of the window however Clem Wallace decided to light a whole pack of sparklers at once causing the sulphur to drip everywhere. We had just recently had a new carpet fitted and there were now big burn marks on it. The next morning Frank Chambers and Billy Budd came in to view the damage. Billy was raging and Frank with his normal laid-back attitude commented, "we'll just have to paint the carpet black to match".

We were not the only ones to misuse pyrotechnics particularly the Mini Flares that the Officers would use for Mini Flare cricket during their socialising back at their Mess. This went terribly wrong on one occasion when an Officer who will remain nameless, caught one in his mouth resulting in him looking the roughest Cavalry Officer you could ever meet. Years later after amalgamation these antics were still going on. On one occasion in Sennelager I was Orderly Sergeant and we had been warned off for a security check Exercise within the next 24 hours. That night I was informed by the Guard Commander that he had heard some bangs from the direction of the Officers' Mess. I went over to investigate to see Mini Flare cricket was in progress and even the Orderly Officer in his Number One Dress was fielding. I let them know how annoyed I was and as I was walking away one of them shouted "Poacher turned Gamekeeper".

Entertainment in the Squadron bar was often quite unexpected. I was walking to tea one evening when I bumped into three strippers who had been booked by the Corporals Mess for a function that night. It was still early, and I managed to persuade them to come up to the bar to do a quick act before going to the Corporals Mess. In no time there was a big circle of chairs, with them in the middle and the more money we gave them the more they performed. By the time they had finished with us they were ready to go home. I directed them to the Cpls' Mess however they certainly did not perform like they had for us. The Cpls were all complaining the next day and wanted a refund.

The NAAFI tried it's hardest to compete against the Squadron bars and every so often would lay on some awful act provided by the "Combined Services Entertainment" Agency. We once had the Group Paper Lace singing "Billy Don't be a Hero" which had been a No1 Hit about 10 years previously. This was about as good as it got. More often than not the comedian would be heckled with shouts of "taxi for the comedian" and one group stormed off complaining that our behaviour was worse than the Paras. They put in a letter of complaint to the RSM when they discovered their microphones had been stuck in the cream gateaux.

Generally, we got on well with the NAAFI staff particularly the females as we were an all-male regiment. The likes of "Manny" and "Bouncy Castle" who would not get a second look anywhere else other than Caen Barracks lines could play hard to get and at times there would be a punch up over them. I certainly had my share of experiences with the female NAAFI staff. I ended up on CO's Orders being demoted from LCpl for waving a sausage between my legs at one of the staff who put in a complaint, to marrying another, which got me promoted to Corporal!

Shortly before I got married we finally had two females posted in as chefs. They arrived on a Sunday afternoon and word soon got around that they would be in the NAAFI bar that evening. The bar was packed for a Sunday night and the normal single rogues were trying their hardest to impress the new girls, however they were soon failing miserably with their behaviour. The girls looked "shell shocked" as at one stage lads were on the pool table shooting the balls out of their backsides into the table pockets. The chefs were accounted for in no time and it was soon back to fighting over "Bouncy Castle".

Although we could all drive 60 tonne tanks many of us did not have a car licence as it was a different category to a tracked vehicle. As a single bloke you were entitled to a trooping flight, which flew to Luton, and you would then have to catch a train to get home. The other method was using the Trans line Coach, which meant sharing with other regiments and it then stopped off at all the major cities in the UK. It really was an horrendous journey. The Regiment purchased its own coach and the PRI drivers like Zac would do return journeys at a reasonable cost, which was fine if you lived in the Midlands but once again it had its limitations. For those who had cars a trip back to UK would cost them next to nothing as they could always find passengers willing to contribute and tax-free fuel coupons were so cheap you didn't care about the cost of filling your car. You could only use the coupons in Germany and the last station at the border to take them was in a place called Wankum. This became a very familiar station and on busy leave periods there would be queues of British Forces Germany (BFG) cars waiting to fill up. The main ferry crossing was Zeebrugge to Dover with some venturing down to Calais for a shorter crossing. When coming back from UK you always left it to the last moment to get back, often travelling in the night and just making first parade in time.

Although Hohne was isolated, cities like Hamburg and Hannover were only an hour away and for those who had cars Denmark was quite a common place to visit. Squadrons sometimes organised trips using the Regimental coach. I managed to get on a trip to Amsterdam with C Squadron. This was my first time and one I'll never forget. It was a good 5-hour journey with lots of drinking on the way. As soon as we arrived there was trouble. Firstly, a Nig (New In Germany) got thrown in the canal and then Andy Burnett thumped a taxi driver who had got out of his car to tell us off as we were blocking his way. We stupidly legged it to a café close by and within no time the Police were outside on horses. They then came in and started arresting all our lot. Me and Robbo quickly moved on to a different table and my little bit of German, "Ich Bin Deutche" saved us. The next morning we were missing quite a few people, including the trip organiser "Gatty" who was still under arrest. We had to return to Hohne without them.

We made the most of being in Germany. One of my favourite memories of a trip away is when we went to the Munich beer festival. Billy Budd organised a mini bus for us through his neighbour who was an RMP Captain. We went and collected it from the RMP station and assured them we would take care of it. Dave Logan agreed to drive and as soon as we got to Munich things went wrong with the mini bus. We were late getting there and could not be bothered to look for a campsite so headed into a multi storey car park. We thought the height barrier was low down to indicate the carpark was closed. Seeing that we could still get in someone lifted the barrier and Logie drove us through. All of a sudden there was a loud scraping noise from the roof of the mini bus. We then realised what the height barrier was! It was only the start of the damage to the bus. Without a care Logie parked up and we headed out for the first night in Munich. The next morning the Germans came in to park up to do their shopping and we were all laying around the car park in our green Army sleeping bags.

The Beer festival starts at 11 in the morning and closes at 11 at night. We were determined to do the duration. By mid-afternoon we were trashed and had to go on the fairground rides to sober up for the evening. It was a great event however the next morning we were to pay the price for such a long drinking session. Logie insisted he was OK to drive, however as we came out of the carpark he caught the wheel arch of the bus on a concrete post. There was now a big dent in the wheel arch as well as big scrape marks on the roof. Logie was sacked from driving before he could do any more damage. On the Monday morning before taking the bus back we tried to conceal the damage by painting the roof of the bus, but there was nothing we could do about the wheel arch. While we were driving it, to hand it back, people kept pointing at the bus. We thought they were pointing at the damage however it turned out we had been dragging a cam net all the way down the road, which somehow had got caught on the towing eye. On arrival at the RMP duty room, once we had disconnected the cam net we then went to apologise to the RMP Captain. It turned out he was upstairs and was now looking down at the bus. He never noticed the different shades of paint on the roof and was quite calm about the wheel arch. We had to pay for the excess but overall got away quite lightly, although it was never available again for QOH.

I did 7 years as a singlie in Hohne with many more tales to tell. During this 7 years we did exercises in Canada and tours to Northern Ireland and Cyprus (which are stories on their own), so life was never dull. Although my generation are sometimes regarded as the "Germany Beer Drinkers" we did play an important role in keeping the Russians on the correct side of the border but above all we were one happy regiment. At 27 it was time for me to get married and start taking my career more seriously. I was lucky to still have a career intact but in those days characters were looked after by Commanding Officers such as Simon Fox. At reunions we reminisce mostly about the single days in Hohne and I'm still reminded of antics which I had forgotten. I will close by thanking all those for the laughs and fun we shared during my single days and I should also apologise to those who got caught up in the trouble which often followed. The Hussars spirit lives on in our reunions.

GEOGRAPHICALLY CHALLENGED.

Picture the scene – At 0900hrs Zulu the Regiment has deployed to Soltau in convoy. Recce troop has sign posted the route to the Release Point (RP). Troop packets move through the RP at twenty minute intervals and then break out, moving tactically to given locations, with each Sabre Squadron having a piece of real estate that it will use prior to moving to defensive positions to provide the Brigade's integrated Direct Fire support. At his Command conference prior to deployment the CO has underlined the importance of all tanks being in hides, cammed up, engines and generators off and on listening watch by 1440hrs. Everything is going well, the Squadrons are firm in location, RHQ Troop is set up with full communications and the CO is walking around RHQ troop. He is in good form and the banter with his soldiers is good. All is well with the world......................well not quite.

At 1450hrs he hears the unmistakeable sound of a Chieftain making its way across the area. 'Who is that?' he asks. 'Not sure Colonel' replies the Int WO. 'Get whoever it is on the air and ask him why the hell he is not in location'. RHQ moves into overdrive and contact is established with the tank commander, but no reason is obtained as to why said tank is not in location. The CO, noted for his ability to blow hotter than the hottest Oxy Acetylene torch in half the time now becomes involved.

"Hello 32A this is 9, where are you? Over."

The noise of Chieftain is getting louder but there is no answer.

"Hello 32A this 9, where are you? Over."

The noise of Chieftain is now annoying the CO even more but still there is no answer. The heat is building!

"HELLO 32A this is 9, where are you? Over."

"32A, I know where I am going but I don't know where I am!"

And the Oxy- Acetylene Torch exploded!!

SANDHURST STAFF DRILL

On the morning prior to Sovereigns Parade at Sandhurst there was (and may still be) a tradition that all those that are not drill instructors attend "Staff Drill." They parade on the main square below Old College and march around in threes doing about turns and salutes to the front and side in front of a drill instructor and watched (from their windows) by Officer Cadets. It has the effects of amusing the Officer Cadets and belittling the staff in front of them. One day, one of the College Sergeant Majors attended. In the front row of the staff squad was a member of the Royal Scots Dragoon Guards (SCOTS DG) who have a yellow zig zag band around their dress hat. In a loud Scottish accent the Sergeant Major shouted, "You! You with the funny hat! Get oot here and tak the squad!"

The SCOTS DG looked around and then pointed at his chest. "Me Sir?"

"Aye! You! Get oot here and let's see some Cavalry drill!" This was said with more than a hint of sarcasm. The Cavalry are not noted for their drill.

The Scots DG marched smartly to the front of the squad, looked at the Sergeant Major and said, "Cavalry drill sir?"

Impatient now the Sergeant Major shouted, "Aye! Get on with it man!"

Turning smartly to the squad the SCOTS DG Sergeant ordered, "Squad, Squad 'shun!" The squad came smartly to attention. "Move to the right in threes, right turn!" The squad, in perfect unison turned smartly to the right. Officer Cadets watched from the windows waiting for the command to step off. The command came.

"Yo!"

How's that for Cavalry drill? Thirty six staff and countless Officer Cadets fell about laughing and a Scots DG made his way to the guardroom! Now that is a man who should transfer in to the Hussars.

FIRE IN THE HOLD

In Fallingbostel 1994 the one thing we dread in the living in blocks occurred over Christmas, a fire in the block. The few soldiers that were in the block managed to get out as the fire took hold. Ancient parquet floors and timbers burned well and it was not long before there was no saving the block. The guard, with their red fire trolley were about as effective as pee on a jet engine and the German fire brigade attended with quite a few fire appliances. In appalling weather, they spent several hours damping down and bringing the fire under control. Although the snow was falling it did not seem much like Christmas for those of A Squadron who had stayed behind for duties.

The following morning the Station Staff Officer attended the scene. The gutted shell of the building looked bleak, but he clearly felt the need for his two pennyworth. "Can't we get a tarpaulin over the roof to keep the snow out to keep it dry?" He asked. The SQMS gave him a withering look and took great pleasure in telling him exactly how many million litres of water the fire brigade had used. The Station Staff Officer retired to lick his wounds!

THE FTX (FULL TROOP EXERCISE).

Once a year (at least into the mid eighties) each brigade conducted an exercise that involved all elements of the Brigade. This was known as the FTX (Full troops Exercise) and each FTX was given a name (Exercise Iron Fist, Crusader, White Rhino etc). Every other year there would be a Divisional FTX where two brigades and support troops would exercise at once. Very occasionally two divisions would exercise and involve up to 30000 troops.

These exercises took place over the German countryside. The last major divisional exercise in which I took part was in 1988. There could be as many as four armoured (Main Battle Tank) regiments, recce, several infantry battalions, engineers, artillery and logistics units deployed into the field (about 400 - 600 armoured vehicles and an equivalent number of wheeled vehicles). Such a concentration of armour, trundling across the North German plain inevitably led to frustrations on behalf of the German population but they understood the reason behind it and were generally supportive.

For the Germans the most important man on the exercise was the claims officer. A troop of tanks could collapse culverts and drainage ditches, destroy roads and fencing (drivers would often spend their evenings cutting wire out of the tanks running gear) and release livestock. There were some unscrupulous farmers who tried it on when making claims therefore the claims officer visited every site for which a claim was made. British troops were often more than happy to help the farmers out. If a farmer had a barn in disrepair he would sometimes ask a tank crew to run over his barn. Done! Good fun! And all of this before the claims for repair of roads and clearing oil spillages from roads and fields.

For the tank crews it was a change from the mud and dust of Soltau. When a squadron pulled into woods and "cammed up" it was not long before the German locals were sightseeing and taking photographs. Track discipline does not cover the fact that a squadron of tanks will destroy miles of woodland paths. We had to keep a close eye on our personal weapons. A few went missing during each major exercise. Most would have dropped off a moving vehicle because a crewman had forgotten it. Some would have been buried or lost in undergrowth, but others disappeared very quickly from where they were last seen and probably ended up in the wrong hands.

Local farmers were pretty good at allowing troops to use their farm buildings. Some would even allow us to use their toilet facilities, once! You could easily make a vehicle disappear in a farmyard. A few plastic sheets and you had a haystack instead of a command vehicle. The farmers were also good for a supply of eggs!

Sometimes the tank crews, being ever alert to the chance of change in diet, would devise ingenious methods to catch food. The odd ducks would disappear, occasionally a chicken. One evening a crew were following a track that went past what appeared to be a small lake. As there were a number of trout lakes in the area the Commander thought of having a fish dinner, lit a thunder flash (a large pyrotechnic that exploded with sufficient force to remove fingers if you were holding it when it went bang), waited for a couple of seconds then threw it into the lake, waiting for it to explode and for the stunned trout to float to the surface ready for "salvage". Not all bodies of water are what they appear to be. When the thunderflash exploded a large plume of liquid covered the tank on the loaders side, covering the loader and seeping into the cam nets and the bins. No trout emerged. The smell that emerged was not even that of fish. It dawned pretty quickly on the crew that the lake had been a pond of farm slurry and waste. In the hide that night the tank was parked 50 yards from the rest of the troop and the crew had to man their own guard and radio watch. The cam nets and the loaders coveralls mysteriously burned the next night.

In the late 70's and through the 80's it was not unusual for German veterans to want to come and look over the tanks. Most were too frail to climb up, but some would share photographs of their time in the Wehrmacht. One showed me pictures of his unit before Stalingrad and then burst into tears as he had been the only one from the unit to return. It was a moving moment. I had no idea what to say and could only nod sympathetically. Other visitors were younger, female and on the pull and some of the crews (single soldiers) were only too willing to show them the turret or the drivers cab and the various buttons and knobs therein.

One element of movement practised on an FTX was a brigade night move. Often this would be over some distance and pass through several towns. It still amazes me that the German population was so understanding. A Chieftain was a noisy beast. Over a hundred of them make a heck of a racket and take a long time to pass. Combine them with a couple of battalions worth of Armoured Personnel Carriers, engineer vehicles and all sorts of other tracked vehicles and the noise went on all night. If the noise was not enough each vehicle had a flashing light, normally very bright. No one on the route can have got any sleep. To top it off the locals would have to negotiate the many broken down vehicles on their way to work the next morning. The Royal Military Police (RMP) put their lives at risk on these moves. They often did not appreciate how much room a tank needs to turn and would have to dive out of the way at the last minute to avoid a sticky ending. We lived in hope. One RMP was left scratching his head when, having recovered from diving out of the way he could see that the tank he had avoided was now embedded into the house on the corner he had been directing traffic round. Nothing could pass in any direction. The tank could not move, despite the protestations of the owner of the house who was in her nightie crying, as it (the tank) was the only thing supporting the house. Everything came to a halt for a long time. Local Police watched on and left it to the RMP to sort out.

On one exercise when I was a commander of a Scimitar in Recce troop I had a new driver. Scimitar was nippy and could achieve 50 mph in the right hands. The new driver had an unfortunate habit of dropping down a gear when moving at full tilt. This had the end result of me being banged around in the turret and almost being thrown out of it. After one really bad gear change I had lost my crew helmet, been thrown forward so violently I had headbutted the smoke grenade dischargers and was bleeding profusely (well I would say that would'nt I?). I managed to get my operator to tell him to stop. I then tied the driver to the back bin of my Scimitar where he stayed for several miles whilst I calmed down and my operator drove. When stopped by a senior officer who asked what I thought I was doing I explained in concise language what had happened and was amazingly told to carry on. The same driver also had a problem telling left from right. "In three hundred yards we are going right." was almost a guarantee that we would go left. Eventually I ordered him out of the drivers cab and made him take off his coveralls. I then told him to tie them to his left wrist and from then on said "Rag" when I wanted him to turn left and "No rag" when I wanted him to turn right. Brilliant. No problems. After a couple of days I relented and once he had got himself dressed again I told him to reverse, said "left stick" and reversed him straight into a tree. I rightfully took a lot of flak. I remembered the shocked face of my own commander several years earlier when I had been a recce troop driver as he had sailed out of the turret past me and landed in a field when I somehow missed the road and come to a sudden halt in a ditch. Nothing changes then.

One of the benefits of being in recce troop whilst on an FTX was we could get away without a lot of supervision as we were usually well in front of the main exercise events. All the troop in 1988 were practical jokers. I was a new comer to the troop when I took over as troop SSgt on Exercise White Rhino and I was driving into the troop hide late. Some of the boys were cooking all in stew, so I drove past and dropped a thunderflash into the pot. Everyone made a dash for it, big bang, no stew. The boys had a plan. They had noticed I was an inveterate scrounger of cigarettes. The next time I scrounged one, Blackie passed it to me with a smile. I should have noticed. As I cupped the cigarette in my hand it blew up. It would do with the insides of a mini flare hidden inside it. Burned my hand, hurt like hell and taught me not to mess with the boys!

That exercise also had one of the most liquid (in terms of alcohol) smokers I can remember. I cannot remember how we managed to get so much beer into our weekend hide but before long cans of beer were being thrown down our necks as if they were belt fed and we had a huge fire going. Not far from us were the Recce troop of the Queens Dragoon Guards who decided they would join us and brought a lot more beer with them. It was only minutes before we were all singing rugby songs and getting totally tanked up. One of the QDG decided to show his party trick of licking a part of his anatomy it is not normally possible to reach. This so impressed one of our Cpls (a Liverpudlian), that he disappeared into the gloom of the night. Occasionally we would see his shadow as he hopped past the fire trying to emulate the feat. He kept trying for hours. I don't know what time the smoker came to an end but the next morning when I woke I could see bodies lying amongst the trees and in the fields surrounding us.

On one of the first exercises I took part in, in Germany, we swam our Scimitars. Early variants of the CVRT range (Scimitar, Scorpion) had a flotation screen. When fully erected it was about six feet high and came to a level about two feet higher than the turret. Provided it had no holes in it, it would hold back the water and the movement of the tracks would propel us (slowly) across the water obstacle. It was not just the flotation screen that had to be prepared. All access plates had to be removed and to have a special, very sticky sealant put around them. Any nut or bolt that gave access to where oil was put in also had to be inspected and correctly sealed. A long exhaust extension was required to take the very hot exhaust above the level of the screen. Get sealant or exhaust extension wrong and you were in trouble.

It was with trepidation that I drove my Scimitar into the water at All Park near Hameln, crossing the river Weser. My commander, Taff Bullock (a really nice guy who looked after me) was calmness itself. I was flapping as all I could see through some plastic coated slits was dirty water getting higher and then the flotation screen pushing toward me as it came under pressure. It held. We moved forward and after what seemed hours began to climb out on the far bank. The next vehicle had a problem as the exhaust extension came off and the exhaust (which got red hot on petrol engine CVRT) started to melt a hole in the flotation screen. Baling out is not how I would describe the frantic activity on the vehicle as it passed half way. Everything was being used to shift water as quickly as possible. They survived. All completely knackered from baling like mad. We looked back at the next vehicle to enter. It was a Stalwart, a six wheeled load carrier. It had a crew of two, commander and driver. The vehicle would enter the water at a steep angle and then level off as it began to float and swim. It was designed to cross water and had water jets to propel it. We noticed things might not be going to plan when the commander reached over from his hatch and began hitting the driver with his radio microphone (the Larkspur system microphone was quite weighty). The next combat indicator was that the Stalwart did not level off but kept going, quite slowly at forty five degrees, like a submarine. Even as it disappeared fully from view the commander was still attempting to brain his driver with the microphone. They both got out, but it took some time to recover the Stalwart.

Rations at that stage comprised of "Compo" rations. These were a range of tinned rations that the Army had been using since before World War 2. They included, Chocolate and Boiled sweets, Cheese, Sausages, Bacon grill, Corned beef, Biscuits, Jam and Burgers and were generally pretty good when topped up with bread, eggs and bacon. At the end of each exercise there was a ritual where married personnel could be seen hopping in and out of the tank park skips to retrieve unused rations. Pay was not great and free tinned food was free food. When one soldier returned from exercise and was bathing at home, his wife, who was new to Germany and military ways asked what he fancied for dinner. The reply was "Furburgers!" It was only when he heard tins rattling that he realised she had not quite picked up the nuance of his reply!

The need for the FTX disappeared as the Berlin Wall came down. Although some exercises continued to take place they were never of the same scale nor did they provide that element of tank soldiering that ensured fun. With their demise the opportunities for such fun became fewer and commanders had to look for more varied methods of keeping tank skills up to speed.

FIJIAN RUGBY

As a young trooper I had joined the Regiment in Warminster. The Regiment had several Fijians serving in it and one of these was my troop Corporal, Joe Luva. The Fijians were hard boys and I had seen with my own eyes Joe launching someone, who had said something he disagreed with, skywards at the end of a rifle butt. I had not met any of the other Fijians by the time we moved to Germany. Shortly after the Regiments arrival in Detmold I played in an inter squadron rugby match. In the second row of the team opposite me was a Fijian. As we scrummed down I put a quick dig through which hit the Fijian. Two very white eyes looked at me and I heard those immortal words, "You're fucking dead!" Suddenly there was no scrum, it had broken apart as the Fijian exploded from it. There was no game of rugby, I and the Fijian were racing away from it at 180 degrees! There was an enormous pain in my side. This Fijian man mountain could move! My entire horizon was taken up by the Fijian as I hit the ground. Boots ran me over and then ran me over again. A hand reached down and grabbed me by the neck and lifted me from the ground. The huge Fijian with no neck looked at me and smiled. "Don't hit me again, cheeky fucker!"

I had met and survived "Tom" Tamani.

NOT QUITE WHAT YOU ASKED FOR

Lt Col (Retd) Paul Hodgson

How many Quartermasters have attended a Commanding Officer's conference to be asked – delete asked, insert ambushed – 'QM, please would you take Tpr Airburst. His Squadron Leader doesn't feel he is best employed in a Sabre Squadron'. The CO knows you will take the lad and so you do. Said soldier was duly transferred to HQ Squadron and came to work for the RQMS, a very senior soldier blessed with management skills that got the best out all who worked for him. Tpr Airbust started to show promise but it was due to fail. Leaving a meeting that seemed to last forever I returned to my office and asked Tpr Airburst to make me a cup of tea. The RQMS who overheard me asked if I would like something to eat. I replied, 'yes please I could murder a NAAFI pie'. The RQ duly obliged and sent our newly acquired young soldier to the NAAFI saying to him 'Young man, here is a good task for you. Go to the NAAFI and get the QM a meat and potato pie from the automated machine. Put it in the microwave next to the machine and then bring it back here pronto." "No problem Sir," and off he dashed. Twenty minutes later Tpr Airbust reported back to the RQ with meal in hand. 'Good lad, take it in to the QM', and he duly did so. Sadly, there was a flaw in the plan. Tpr Airburst had indeed gone to the NAAFI and taken a pie from the automated machine and then put it in the microwave, however that is where the plan went wrong. What he had not been told was to take the white plastic knife and fork off the top of the pie before putting it in the Microwave!! Sometimes soldiers just don't fit in any Squadron!

THE BLACK PIG

Tanks in D Squadron have carried the symbol of a black Pig for a number of years now and I have heard all sorts of reasons why ranging from the capture of a pig during WW2 to a Vietnamese pot bellied pig belonging to an ex SSM.

Much like the story of charge of The Scots Greys during the battle of Waterloo the truth is much less glamorous. The famous Black Pig is a result of a night of revelry by D Squadron QOH personnel in Detmold in the very early 80's. Some drunken members of the squadron came upon a black plastic pig outside a bank (The Dresdener I think) in the town centre and liberated it to the squadron bar where it became a trophy of note and eventually a squadron mascot. One individual then painted a pig on his tank and this was followed by other commanders. The birth of a tradition!

BATUS – 70's -90's.

MCCP. The RAFs way of getting revenge for the fact that we had great fun getting down and dirty on exercise and they had to sleep in heated hotels! Movement Control Check Point. Any normal person would tip up for a flight about two hours before it was due to take off. This is clearly not enough for the movers of the RAF, Crab Air. A movement using a Crab Air arranged flight starts some 24 hours before the plane is due to take off. Report, check kit, check paperwork, bugger off. Come back again. Check kit, check paperwork. Hang around. Check kit, check paperwork, get on buses to the point of departure. Check kit, check paperwork. Hang around. All this palaver being "controlled" by someone with a large wagon wheel badge on their arm. Rank, SAC (Senior aircraftsman). With no respect for the rank of the people they were addressing these "wagon wheels" made movement from A to B about as complex and painful as it could possibly be made.

Having managed to successfully navigate MCCP we board a flight at RAF Gutersloh destined for Calgary in Canada, on our way to Exercise Medicine Man (EX MED MAN). In the seventies and eighties the Regiment managed at least one EX Med Man a year and sometimes two. All of us, except for the very new troopers knew what was in store. The aircraft (a VC10) took off, levelled off and headed for Canada. Some of the Squadron were taking clandestine sips from water bottles that contained anything but water. The cabin quickly filled with smoke fumes and ash trays rapidly filled. After about an hour the air was so thick with smoke that your eyes hurt and half the Squadron was looking half cut. If you tried to go to sleep it was inevitable that just as you dropped off an RAF air steward would wake you and ask if you wanted a drink or hand you a meal in a silver foil tray (usually pretty good food). Sometimes we stopped off at Keflavik in Iceland so the plane could refuel and we could conduct our own replenishment with Carlsberg. The onward eight hour flight seemed to pass very slowly. Those that had managed to have an alcoholic drink in their water bottles had usually managed to sleep and sober up by the time of arrival in Canada. We were shepherded into a fleet of American style buses and then began the two and a half hour drive to BATUS, The British Army Training Unit Suffield. This drive in the buses was the first sight we got of the prairies. For those that had not been before the very fact that there was nothing to look at was interesting. We peered out of the windows, hoping to catch a glimpse of a Bison or a Wolf or even Cochise..............but nothing. The view of a sea of grass was occasionally broken by a petrol (gas) station or roadside diner. By the time the coaches turned off the Trans Canada highway and headed for Suffield it was clear that this was a very different environment in which to train.

Climbing down from the buses, the Squadron was paraded, given a quick brief on the camp and then set to work. We unloaded masses of boxes and weapon bundles from the buses and from a huge Mack truck that had followed. Then we were taken to our accommodation and shown where the wash and toilet blocks were. These blocks were usually about as far as you could possibly get from the accommodation blocks without requiring transport. A hotel this was not. We were accommodated in long wooden huts, about sixty to a hut (later replaced by H block style concrete accommodation blocks). We had a bed. Either the top or bottom of a bunk bed and that was it. Our kit was in our kit bags and large packs. We were told where the cookhouse was and the meal timings and told where the junior ranks bar was. Once you had managed to get a bed space you took your first look at the country side surrounding the camp. Grass. Some cactus. Gophers. Look left and you could see the dust bowl (where all the tanks pulled up and loaded prior to going out on the prairie and de-kitted on return) and workshops areas. Look right and, in the middle distance, about a mile and a half, the town of Ralston. With nothing much to do the obvious place to go was the junior ranks club.

The junior ranks club was not the place for a pacifist. If you were lucky and on one of the first flights you could have a relatively peaceful first night but as the Battle Group began to arrive in numbers, the small club (another wooden hut) became overwhelmed. You bought beer in bulk (because you had to wait an age to get served) and drank outside, sitting on the wooden benches that were weathered and splintered. Members of your Regiment, Gunners, a couple of Infantry Battalions, sappers, Ordnance Corps, REME all mixing in a confined space and all with access to a lot of beer. Trouble was frequent, usually started by Coco or some other clown throwing the beer bottle he had just paid for at you. If the weather was cold or wet then everyone crammed inside. Trouble was less frequent because you could not move. On one early Med Man one of the Infantry mobs was 4 RRF (Royal Regiment of Fusiliers), all Geordies. They could not understand Brummies and the Regiment could not understand them. Both therefore presumed the other was being a prat and retaliated at the first word.

On the first morning you woke early, at about four o'clock because your body clock was screwed. By breakfast you were tired again. Then began the briefings. Royal Military Police brief. The usual "We are here to help you" which was in fact true but always taken with a pinch of salt. "Do not upset the RCMP (Royal Canadian Mounted Police) because they are robust in their policing methods." "Do not touch any girl under the age of 16 because it is statutory rape." "Do collect your condoms from the guardroom before going down town." (They really did have condoms in the guardroom. They were more like colanders because each guard commander in turn would spend the night piercing them with pins.) "Do not upset the local Canadians who have seen hundreds of different Regiments and Battalions, have survived them all and are generally harder than you are!" All true. Completely ignored.

R+R Brief (Rest and Recuperation brief) telling us what was available at the end of the exercise over a specific four day period. There were numerous activities ranging from sort it out yourself to adventure training in the Rockies, to ranching to organised trips to Vancouver and golfing tours. Most hired a cab from the local rent a wreck (and they really were wrecks!) or bought local BATUS bangers, cars that were passed on from Battlegroup to Battlegroup (or Combat Team or Taskforce, whatever the "In" terminology of the day was).

The brief we were all interested in was from the Quarter Master Technical about how we would take over and more importantly handover our tanks. This was always done with lots of swearing and numerous promises of death and destruction if anything went wrong. We would take over complete crap and we would handover tanks off the back decks of which you could eat a meal. This was the format for all handover takeovers. You ALWAYS took over crap because the Regiment you were taking over from was rubbish, but you ALWAYS handed over the best tanks because you were, without a doubt, the BEST Regiment that there was. As vehicle commanders from the different battlegroups you did not argue with each other but contacted the relevant Quarter Master Technical (QM Tech) to point out any hassles. He linked up with his counterpart, had a coffee, reached into the magic bag and brought out an item that solved the argument. All Quarter Masters had a magic bag, very much like that carried by Mary Poppins but this one contained tanks, and spares and people and lots of machine gun rear mounting pins!

On the day of the takeover all the tanks were lined up, tool kits on the ground in front of them. The commander taking over would conduct a tool check. This was almost a completely pointless exercise because as soon as an item was called and shown to the commander taking over it was spirited away and passed down the back of the line of tanks until it reached a vehicle where the crew had lost one of those items. It was then laid out in their tool kit and the whole process would be repeated. Very rarely did a crew handing over have missing tools. Very rarely did a crew taking over have a complete tool kit. However, it was a system that worked.

Once the tanks were taken over they were moved onto the dust bowl where they were lined up with the rest of the Regiment in squadron lines and preparation for the exercise would begin. The crews that had handed over would disappear on their R+R. Those of us about to deploy would work on the vehicles during the day and then, in the evenings visit the town of Medicine Hat, about twenty miles away.

The usual means of transport to Medicine Hat was taxi. You always shared in order to spread the cost. There were always lots of willing volunteers to share. There was sometimes a coach or some trucks laid on. These did a return trip that left "The Hat" at about midnight on the way back.

There were a number of different bars in Medicine Hat. The Silver Buckle, Cadillacs and Cheetahs were three that were visited by good numbers of soldiers on a regular basis but the most famous (or infamous) watering hole was the "Sin Bin" (Assiniboia Inn). This was ostensibly a hotel and people did stay there but when a Battlegroup was in town I doubt anyone actually slept there less those who were sleeping "It" off. One large, long bar in a large, long room. It served beer by the jug (usually holding about 4 pints). You went to the bar, bought your jug then threw it down you neck as quickly as you could. Several jugs later you started on the spirits. If you were very drunk your friends would put you on the transport back to Suffield at midnight. If you were very drunk but still able to stand you carried on and risked the wrath of Sergeant Majors the following morning. Fights and full scale bar brawls were common. A few girls frequented the place but usually they left fairly early, often with squaddie in tow. One thing nearly all the watering holes had in common were strippers. These young ladies would dance in a specific area and those watching would try to stuff rolled up bank notes into the knickers or bras of the dancer. Gradually clothing was removed until there was a loud cheer as all was revealed, only for the stripper to run off, get dressed and start all over again ten minutes later. There were some really VERY pretty ladies, there were some ladies who were recognised as having been in various publications not for sale in the UK and there were some real dogs. In the early evening the squaddies would usually let them know which category they came into. By ten at night they were all beautiful as the squaddies were by now wearing Heineken glasses.

The following morning Company and Squadron Sergeant Majors paraded their Squadrons. Inevitably there were those with black eyes and various wounds. As they were clearly defending the honour of the Regiment no action was taken but there were, also inevitably those that were going to wake up in one of the Sin Bins rooms next to a girl they did not know with not enough money to get back. Massively frowned upon. They were usually gated (confined to the camp), paraded behind the guard in the evenings and given various extra duties such as sweeping the dust bowl with a toilet brush. Eventually they were put in front of the Commanding Officer and fined or jailed on their return to their base in UK or Germany. Clap was also a rare but not unheard of punishment for those late nights in "The Hat". There were however occasions when a squaddie was absent because he was in hospital having been the victim of local hoods. One such event happened in the late 80s when a member of a Scottish Battalion was beaten to within an inch of his life by some locals with baseball bats. Others had been with the victim and could identify the culprits. The Company Sergeant Major had a quiet word with the Regimental Sergeant Major and several four ton trucks were arranged for the following evening. Of course, the RSM subsequently knew nothing of any plans. The company paraded, moved to "The Hat" and entered the bar the assault had occurred in. The doors were locked behind them and guarded. The Mounties (RCMP), being wise and just, as well as robust, waited outside. After several minutes the bar doors were opened and five very bruised individuals gladly handed themselves over to the RCMP. The RMP looked the other way.

The day before deployment was very busy with members of the Squadron visiting the dustbowl then stores then dustbowl then armouries and then back to dustbowl. All tools were checked again. Guns and breeches checked. Obturators fitted. Spare ones checked. Cam nets rolled into long thin tube shapes and draped around the turret. Personal kit in large packs loaded. Cookers double checked. Unused charge bins filled with cream soda or Labatts Blue. Canvas water carriers known as Chaguls were filled. Tank sheets on. Shower (you probably would not see a shower or toilet for at least ten days) and then attempt to sleep.

The journey out of camp always seemed endless. You sat in your turret or drivers cab watching the other squadrons go out, lines of 432 Armoured Personnel Carriers trundle slowly past, their petrol engines coughing and spluttering. Centurion bridge layers, Centurion Armoured Recovery Vehicles, endless red topped land rovers and Ferret scout cars and then, when there was more dust in the air than that thrown up by Icelandic volcanos it was your turn. On my first few BATUS exercises I was a gunner so avoided most of the dust. Later as commander of 24B I was last in the B Squadron line as we left the dustbowl. Before I had gone fifty yards I was black with dust and had grit in every orifice. By the time I had travelled a hundred yards I had passed the first broken down Chieftain. Then every mile or so you passed another vehicle with its yellow flag up, waiting for the REME to come and fix them. I trundled along quite nicely for a couple of hours until I got to a place called Wells Junction when something hit me very hard in the chest then kicked me in the nose. Once I could clear my eyes I saw that it was my gunner standing on the turret in front of me and that smoke was filling the turret. It must have taken him no little effort to twist round in his super confined seat and propel himself through the tiny gap between my legs and the even tinier gap between me and the rest of the Commanders cupola. Funny what fear can do. I was not amused as I grabbed the radio and told my Squadron Leader that I had a fire on board. My gunner stood sheepishly on the back decks. As it turned out it was not a fire but a loose fuel filter allowing diesel to spill onto hot engine components that had generated enough smoke to flood into the turret. Neither my loader nor I had noticed as we had our heads out of the turret, but my gunner had certainly noticed. I would have preferred a tug on my coverall trouser legs rather than a boot in the chest as he went past me. It was not until after dark that we were fixed and could re-join the Squadron. The Squadron was a few miles away at the start point for one of the early exercises, "Burrowing Owl". A few miles across country does not sound like a major obstacle until you take the following into account. Night in Canada is as black as you can possibly paint night. There is no ambient light unless the Northern Lights are showing. GPS or the Global Positioning System was something you saw on Star Trek and to read the map you had to shine a torch which completely screwed up any night vision you might have had. There are not that many hills (if you could see them) so there are not many contour lines on the map. At one point I stopped the tank so that I could jump off and take a compass bearing. You had to be away from the tank as a large lump of metal near you is not great when taking bearings. I jumped off and immediately sank to my knees in cold water. After a little investigation I realised I had managed to stop my tank right on the edge of the only substantial lake on this part of the prairie, Andersons Lake. A few more feet could have been disastrous. By some miracle I eventually arrived with the Squadron and the crew and I grabbed what sleep we could on the back decks.

The first few exercises were designed to develop crew skills in stages. You started with a machine gun exercise with just your tank and built up to troop and squadron exercises with your attached Infantry platoon. It was always, ALWAYS, better to be with your squadron than to be detached to an Infantry company. The Infantry had no idea of what comfort was and had no idea how much oil and fuel a Chieftain could consume. Worse still, some Infantry companies were dry (no alcohol)! It was on one of these warm up exercises that I had the bright idea of using my contra rotation. This device unlocked the commanders cupola (a small turret with the machine gun on it) from the rest of the turret allowing the commander to scan an area of ground different to that of his gunner. OK when static but using it when moving, particularly when acting as "intimate support" (tanks going in to the attack with the Infantry) is not recommended. My hull was going one way, my turret another and my cupola another. "Left stick! No! Traverse left! Bollocks! Traverse right! Driver are you thick?" (unprintable reply ending in "dick head".) "Stop!" I wanted to throw up. How I ended up in the correct place I do not know. To be complimented by the safety staff who followed us in was nothing short of miraculous considering I could have run them over and not known about it. If any of you have ever sat in a spinning cup at a fair ground this was MUCH worse. These progressive exercises continued until you were ready for the full regimental exercise, Exercise Salamanca.

Map reading in BATUS is tough. There were navigational aids to assist commanders in finding their way around. The 1980's equivalent of GPS was a wooden tower in the middle of nowhere with a large wooden coke can on it. This was, fairly originally, named Coke Can tower. There was a Banana tower and an X ray tower and numerous other towers. Fine and dandy during the day. Every night the Squadron Quarter Master Sergeant (SQMS) would travel out from the main camp with your "replen" (fags, booze, food, fuel, in order of priority). To find us he often had to travel significant distances and he had never heard of GPS either. As it was dark the towers were of little use unless he ran into one. His map reading had to be spot on. Hmmm. Chieftain was equipped with two navigational aids. These were the commanders spotlight (about as powerful as a car headlight on dipped beam) and the searchlight. This was no little affair. It was housed in a large metal container on the side of the turret and could illuminate targets a good couple of kilometeres away. When one or other crew called up on the radio to say that they were lost one of his troop would first shine a torch. If this was not successful, the spotlight would be used. "Shining now." he would report and shine the spotlight heavenward. As light was visible for miles at night this was usually sufficient to lead the errant vehicle into the leaguer from several miles away, but not always. One SQMS got himself completely lost. When he had failed to see a torchlight and had then failed to see the spotlight the decision was made to shine the searchlight. It was probable that this could be seen from space. It could not be seen by the SQMS. It was going to be a VERY long night.

At the end of each day the Squadron would make its way to the start of the next day's activities and then go into a box leaguer. Prior to the final Battlegroup exercise, once in the leaguer life became "non Tac". Maintenance could be done in the open, there was no need to put up the cam nets and a beer or two could be cracked. If it was hot weather, you could wear shorts order (PT shorts and boots). When the PPCLI (Princess Patricia's Canadian Light Infantry) were attached to us we were amazed to see a truck pull up, a screen dropped down the side of the vehicle and a movie put on. Another truck arrived and set up a BBQ. The majority of the Squadron made their way over and a good night was had by all.

Whether the leaguer was "non tac" or not there was one unwritten but very important rule. The Bivi's (sleeping shelters of whatever type) went up on the inside of the leaguer and they all went up on the same side of the vehicles. No one but no one drove any sort of vehicle down the inside of the leaguer without a guide on the ground. People had previously been killed by vehicles driving over their tents. Tanks would often come into the leaguer after dark and although you knew there was someone on the ground making sure it went nowhere near your shelters it was still a frightening experience to listen to the sound of tracks rumbling only inches from your head. If you knew vehicles would be coming into the leaguer late at night the crew would often prefer to sleep on the back deck of their vehicles, an option not available to the Infantry. Another thing you did not do was sleep under the vehicle. Tanks could, and often did settle into the soil, particularly when it was wet. No one would hear you being crushed to death.

As the exercise entered its final stages and the battlegroup came together, "non tac" nights became a thing of the past. Sentries were deployed at all stops. Ground sentry, NBC sentry, air sentry and radio watch ensured that sleep was at a premium for the troop. Cam nets had to be put up whenever you stopped for any length of time. The normal european style cam net was a nightmare to put up, catching on everything it could do. The cam nets used in BATUS were so very much worse. Hessian stitched to a mesh of twine it collected every bit of dust on the prairie (which turned to concrete when it rained) and seemed to weigh more than the tank it was covering. It caught on everything. The only things that were strong enough to hold the net off the turret so that you could move around the tank were the wooden gun cleaning staves. If you failed to wedge them in properly or the wind got up the staves would slip and fall, often hitting crew in the process. I hated Canadian cam nets. It was difficult trying to hide on the prairie.

When it was difficult to hide a tank, it was equally difficult to have privacy when going to the toilet. You grabbed your converted oil drum (bottom and top cut off and masking tape around the rim for comfort) and wandered off looking for a dip in the terrain. When you found one a hole was dug, the drum was placed over the hole and you sat. It was always safer to use your converted drum than try to sit on any of the few natural features such as small piles of rocks. After a particularly loud scream, one crewman (who had not taken a drum) came running into the leaguer shouting, "I've been bit, I've been bit!" and he then lay down on the ground butt up. Sure enough, there were two little puncture holes about three quarters of an inch apart on his cheek. Clearly he had been rattled! (Rattle snakes are not rare on the prairie). Whether it was this individuals place in the popularity stakes or not is unknown but a queue of friends willing to suck the poison out did not materialise! Remarkably quickly a helicopter arrived and whipped him away to Medicine Hat hospital where an antidote was administered. He was back with the Squadron within a couple of days.

Training at BATUS allowed us to do things that were not possible in the UK or Germany. For the night firing phase of the exercise the tanks pulled up on a ridge line overlooking some old tanks used as targets. There was no thermal imagery so you had to wait for the gunners or mortars to put up illumination before you could fire. The illumination provided just enough light to see hard targets by out to about fifteen hundred metres. One troop leader who took on a night shoot managed to shoot one of the Infantry 432 APCs. Despite firing only a Sabot training round of mild steel it blew the drivers hatch some 300 feet into the air and passed straight through the 432. Luckily the crew had earlier been evacuated from the vehicle as it had broken down. The illuminated arc marker had been hung on the rear of the vehicle, leaving most of it "in arc" and therefore fair game. Despite the obvious fury of all the hierarchy and a suspicion that the troop leader had known exactly what he was aiming at nothing could be done.

Chieftain could also perform semi indirect fire out to a range of ten kilometres. The gunner had a clinometer to his left and by using a number of calculations, the readings of which were applied to the clinometer, the barrel could be elevated until the bubble in the clinometer was level (similar to a spirit level). Once you fired it was a surreal feeling waiting for what seemed like an age but was really only about thirteen seconds, before you saw your round impact on the ground ten kilometres away.

The last part of the final exercise was always the breaching of a minefield followed by an obstacle crossing and then a deliberate attack. All great fun but the really impressive bit of kit in use was the engineers "Giant Viper". This was a length of explosive hose, about a hundred metres long, that was fired out of its trailer by rockets and then exploded as it hit the ground, in theory exploding or moving all the mines in its path. There was a huge bang when it went off and a hundred metre long explosion is a thing of beauty! Through the minefield gap we would all drive and then make our way into either overwatch or a Forming up Point (FUP). The overwatch tanks would open fire on the objective, the attacking tanks and Infantry would burst out from the FUP and attack and we would win. Endex.

Endex was followed by recovery from the Prairie and handover to the next Battle Group. Recovery could take many hours but eventually the tanks pulled into the dust bowl to de-kit and get rid of any major gunge and would then progress through the washdown, where every bit of mud and dust was washed off them and then into the servicing bay. There they would be fully serviced. The tank would then move onto the vehicle park where tool checks were completed and you cleaned the tank until it was spotless. You did not go back to the accommodation. You worked on the vehicle until it was ready. Then you could go for a shower and rest before going back to the vehicle park to assist other crews and wait until your vehicle was inspected by the REME. You collected your missing tools by stealing them from other units (non Hussars) or asking the Quartermaster Technical to reach into his magic bag. Then you handed your tank over to the rubbish battlegroup that was taking over.

R+R could take many forms. I tried ranching first. This turned out to be one of the most painful experiences of my life. I had blisters inside my thighs, in the crack of my bottom and in the small of my back. My legs were stiff for an age and my thumb was completely knackered as I twice hit it with a huge hammer as my ranching experience consisted of riding one of the local ranch owner's nags around his boundary fences repairing his wiring along with a Canadian (who I thought was mute so little did he talk) and a Geordie Fusilier. Four days of complete purgatory. The next time I went on R+R I went to Vancouver. I never got to Vancouver because

I got completely plastered in Banff and slept through the rest of the Rockies. On other occasions I visited Calgary, Medicine Hat, Edmonton and Lethbridge all of which have lots of bars. Calgary also has Canadian soldiers who I took great pleasure in winding up. A fight started but just as it started a friend wrapped his arms around me from behind shouting, "don't hit him!" and would not let go. The Canadian therefore took his time in using my face as a punch bag. I attacked my friend.

Arriving back after R+R we were told to keep away from members of the incoming battlegroup and barred from going down to Medicine Hat. We had to endure another MCCP (always quicker on the way back) and then it was time to get on the buses and start the long journey back to Hobart Barracks in Detmold where contact with the local bars was resumed.

A BUM WRAP

The end of a long days firing and then a long drive to the night location. "Bear" driving and "Big Dave" operating. The turret full of ammunition ready for another days firing tomorrow. Big Dave was asleep, head and shoulders on one side of the loaders hatch and large bottom on the other. The hatch was almost vacuum sealed! Bear was getting tired. The tank had been purring across the prairie for hours. Bear did not see the large rock that he hit and that jolted the tank so hard that big Dave was rapidly forced into the turret and landed on the ready racks bum first. The ready racks were full of Sabot. Maybe not as sharp as Fin stabilised sabot but sharp enough to penetrate almost anything............It was a bum wrap and a painful one!

Typical BATUS terrain. It was unforgiving to poor map reading.

An armoured Battlegroup in the mid 90's.

THE DINNER NIGHT – WARRANT OFFICERS AND SERGEANTS MESS – 1986

Its half past five. Two hours to go until we have to be in the Mess. Dinner nights costs a fortune! Long dress and make up for the wife, Mess Dress dry cleaned after the last mess night. All before we get any sort of bill for the function.

It's going to be a levy night tonight. That means that the total cost is split between all the mess members evenly. It sounds fair but when you consider half the cost is alcohol and fags it is'nt fair on those that do not smoke or only drink a little. The unfairness of a levy night has been raised endless times at mess meetings but RSM after RSM has ignored it. If you dare to raise it the majority of the mess, who all drink like fish and smoke like chimneys stare at you as if you're some sort of slime that has just climbed out of a drain. I have never been stared at. I love a levy night! Free fags and loads of booze (most of which gets left on the tables and then washed down the drain or the necks of the Corporals who are forced to wait on. Does'nt matter. Just get another one!)

Time to get dressed. The wife's been going at it since five. Painting her face. Nice undies for afterwards! I'm on a promise! I slip into my Mess dress trousers and pull them up to my waist. Phew! They still fit (ish). Mess dress trousers are tight! I can't do them up yet as once they are up you can't bend properly to put your socks and George boots on. Trousers round your ankles, the socks go on. Then you check your boots and make sure that your spurs are going to stay in. Your supposed to have box spurs (they just click into a recess in your boot) but most try to get screw in spurs as they do not come off. Spurs are expensive and sometimes silly buggers try to nick them when you are sitting at the table. Spurs on, boots on, trousers up. I have a white collarless shirt. It has no collar because the mess dress waistcoat has a collar that is so tight you cannot do it up if you have a collar on your shirt. Braces on. Waistcoat next. Zipped up at the side it held most of me in! It has two hook and eye attachments at the back of the collar that force the collar around your neck. It rubs like mad, itches all night and the next day your neck is red raw. Traditions hurt. Then the jacket. If you're lucky you got a jacket with a pocket and you can get your lighter in. Where are my medals? Most of us have the General Service medal for Northern Ireland. A few have Long Service and Good Conduct medals. If you had a Cyprus medal as well, you were legend. Three medals! Amazing!

The wife is pushing it. "Should I wear these earrings or these?" "Is my make up right?" "The dress has a pull in it!" "Do these shoes go? I NEED more shoes!"

Coming out of the flat we see lots of other senior NCOs in their mess dress, some looking every bit as uncomfortable as I am, others looking as if their collars fit them like a glove. A pile of fag ends is already building up around the group. As we approach, the wives look each other up and down. Some thinking that they had been outdone, others sneering because so and so had worn that same dress two dinner nights ago. Did the dress reach down to the shoes? Long dress means long dress! Bus in to camp. All the blokes saying they were not going to drink too much as they had to do this or that the next day. Pulling up outside the mess fingers went into collars to try and make them looser and the girls all looked at their powder compacts to make sure their make up was immaculate.

Into the mess through the double doors. Two waiters with trays of drinks. "Hello mate!" It's my troop corporal. "Get you a beer later" said with a knowing wink. The trays are full of wine glasses, half red, half white. Another Corporal is holding a tray of soft drinks and a few of the ladies go for these. Walking into the mess you see you have arrived at about the same time as the majority of the mess members (all SNCO were mess members) and the bar is crowded. NO ladies at the bar! No ladies within six feet of the bar! Not allowed. If a lady goes to the bar to get a drink you get extra duties. There are strict codes in the mess.

The ladies gather in groups in the ante room whilst you get the first beer of the night down your neck. There is about half an hour to go before the dinner night starts proper. That wine was nice! Another glass of that will go down well. "Pete! Grab us another pint!", you shout as you seek out the waiter. Your wife wants another drink and is trying to catch your eye. She gives up and grabs another glass of wine. Not a Malibu but it will do for now.

Glass of wine in one hand and beer in another most of the others are similarly encumbered by drinks. Promises of sobriety have quickly gone out of the window! Not too much booze though, I am on a promise! Squadron Sergeant Majors wander around chatting to their Troop Sergeants. Troop Sergeants chat to one another. The wives form groups and chat to one another. A group of Squadron Sergeant Majors wives hover around the RSMs wife. The odd Sergeant's wife tries to ease into the group but is ignored so she wanders back over to the group of Sergeant's wives she was chatting to earlier.

In the background there is a blast of music. Five minute warning! Bugger! I still have a pint! I'll neck it quick and still have time for the loo before we go into the dining area. Twenty five minutes I've been in here and still only a couple of glasses of wine and two pints. Not bad. You had to make the toilets because you were not allowed to leave during the meal or the speeches that followed that could go on for hours! Have to watch it though. Don't want to get pissed too soon. The bogs are crowded. I just make it back out in the five minutes. As I leave the toilets there is another blast of music and the band strikes up. Find the wife. Where's the bloody WIFE! Oh, there you are. I smile endearingly (I think) as she gives me a look that says you have not said a word to me since we walked in. Check the seating plan, a diagram of where everyone is sitting that takes the President of the Mess committee (PMC) weeks to prepare. There are three long legs and another leg that goes across the top of the three legs. This is the top table. RSM, ASM (the senior member of the LAD and also a Warrant Officer 1st Class), RQMS' then the SSMs. Motor Transport Warrant Officer and Regimental Signals Warrant Officer usually do not fit so they go the top of one of the adjoining legs close to the top table. The three long legs are filled in order of seniority. The more senior you are the closer to the top table you are placed. I only had to look at the bottom of the legs as I had only been a Sergeant for a couple of years.

There we are. Middle leg, right hand side. I was seated with my wife on my left and another Sergeants wife on my right. It always went boy, girl, boy, girl. To my wife's left was Mr Vice, the most junior Sergeant. He had to say grace. He had clearly been in the bar practicing for some time, he was already bladdered!

Everyone was in. The PMC looked around to ensure there was silence. "Mr Vice!" came the command.

Mr Vice looked down at the piece of paper he was holding and staggered slightly before regaining his composure. "Blesh us Oh Lord and all theshe gits, wish we are about to reshieve from...... from..........amen!" A muted snigger ran around the mess. Poor lad had only been promoted a few weeks ago. The RSM gave Mr Vice an icy stare. It was clear from that look that when "Mr Vice" was invited into the RSMs office on the Monday morning it would be a short, one way conversation. Luckily this Mr Vice was single so escaped an immediate ear bending from a stricken wife. Time to sit down. I reached for the chair of the lady to my right and pulled it out so that she could sit down. Mr Vice reached for my wife's chair and fell over. He then grabbed the chair as he got back to his feet and managed to pull it out for my wife. "Get off you fool!" she said with a quiet venom that brought a sobered look to his eyes immediately. We all sat, my wife looking at me in disbelief. To her left Mr Vice had gone to sleep.

The first course was already on the table. A fish starter. The mess steward helpfully ensured that the cutlery was laid out in the order in which it was used. Not only did this look good but prevented complete novices from eating fish with the wrong knife and fork. It looked wonderful, but my wife was watching Mr Vice as he slowly slid from his chair. The mess steward with the help of two Corporals also helpfully removed drunks.

A host of corporals then appeared dressed in green barrack dress trousers and cream shirts, carrying bottles of wine. These were the wine waiters. For those that had to wait on (serve the SNCOs) wine waiter was the favoured job. No chance of dropping food and every chance of necking the bottles when out of sight. They moved along the seated masses serving over the right shoulder. Several of the Sergeants quietly told the wine waiters not to ask if they wanted a drink but just to keep them topped up. Wine served, first course finished and another mass of waiters appeared. They had all been in the mess an hour or so before the doors had opened to the mess members and they had practised where to stand and who to serve. They had then waited and waited some more. Some of the wine disappeared, usually quite a lot of it! Now they removed the plates and cutlery that had been used and then brought out another course. Whilst all this hectic action was taking place the mess members drank and chatted and the band played various medleys. It was fantastic having your own band playing for you. The hot meal was delivered to the top table first and then delivered in rank order until those at the bottom of the long legs got theirs. Once everyone had been served the PMC gave the RSM the nod and he picked up his cutlery. That was the signal for everyone else to eat. The wine waiters came out again and filled glasses to the brim. Some of the wine waiters were beginning to show signs of wear and tear, in fact several of the food waiters were showing signs of wear and tear as well! The whole process was repeated, and the final course was delivered to the tables. Wine waiters again. I was beginning to regret the two pints of beer I had so foolishly drunk before coming into the dining room. Music. Listen to the music. The band had now started a session of entertainment that included solo acts. These boys were good. It was coming soon now, one of the favourite parts of any dinner night. A long post horn was brought out and one of the seated SNCOs invited to get up and play. This was a band SNCO who knew how to play the crowd. Grabbing the instrument, he began to play the post horn gallop. As he played he placed the horn next to people's ears or pretended to offer it to them so they could have a go. Occasionally he did pass the horn across and inevitably a feeble raspberry sound would emit. Then horn away and out came a kettle. He played the post horn gallop on the kettle and then, wonder of wonders, on a toilet. These boys were good! More wine waiters. Ouch! A couple of the ladies were laughing further down the more senior end of the table. It appeared that one of the Staff Sergeants had relieved himself into a bottle. Elsewhere a chair was removed from the table. A Sergeant had crawled out of the room in a vain attempt to get to the toilets unnoticed. Not a chance. Those sitting nearest to where he had been had, as soon as he had crawled out, taken his chair and passed it down the table. All he could do on his return was pretend to sit but after a few seconds the pain of assuming the sitting position without a chair (and the effects of alcohol) became too much and he had to acknowledge the fact that he was going to get extra duties. The PMC was also informed of the man who had relieved himself into a bottle. One of the wives then got up and walked to the toilet quite openly. Husband? Unlucky, he got extras because he could not control his wife.

The final course was taken away and the wine waiters then came and removed everyone's wine glasses. A few tried to hide them, but they were taken anyway. More wine waiters appeared standing behind the RSM and at intervals along the various legs. The held decanters full of port which were eventually placed down on the tables. Once the RSM began to pour his glass everyone else began to pour. The custom was to pass the port to the right. Some people poured the glass of the person next to them, some poured the port without allowing the base of the decanter to leave the table. In the end everyone had port. The PMC would then stand. "Ladies and Gentlemen, please be upstanding and join me in the Loyal Toast." Scraping of chairs as everyone stood up. "The Queen!" Everyone repeated "The Queen!" First sip of port, more scraping of chairs as everyone sat down. Almost immediately there was another toast. Scraping of chairs. "The Regiment!" "The Regiment!" was the loud reply. After which there was a short period of relaxation before the RSM stood to give his speeches. During this pause silver cigarette boxes full to the brim with cigarettes were placed on the tables and the majority of the mess lit up. It was not a healthy atmosphere for a non-smoker.

Dinner nights were usually held to mark the fact that a long standing member of the mess was leaving the Regiment to become a civilian. Someone, usually a friend would go through his entire military life, and often his life before he joined the Army and dig up as much dirt as possible. This was then passed to the RSM. The aim was not to belittle the person leaving but to inform, in an amusing way, tales of his daring do and most amusing cock ups. As the RSM spoke there was generally silence but on the odd occasion someone would heckle and get out of hand. Their names were noted. More for the RSMs office on Monday morning. The individual who was leaving was then invited to reply and state how much he and his wife had loved their time in the Regiment. The wife would then be presented with a bouquet of flowers and the soldier with whatever he had agreed to be presented with. Usually to do the speech and listen to the reply was about fifteen minutes. Tonight, there were two people being dined out. I am seriously going to wet myself! This is agony! The thirty minutes seemed to take weeks. There was a general uncomfortable shuffling amongst the mess, including the ladies. Another speech and there was going to be a monsoon! Luckily speeches were over. Music began. Stirring regimental marches. For those attached to the mess it was good if they knew their own regimental march as they were expected to stand up for it (cost a round of drinks if they failed, expensive with over a hundred people in the mess). The Physical Training Corps music played. A set of legs then appeared at the dining table being waved around in military fashion by the instructor doing a handstand at the table (PT corps tradition). One instructor even walked down the table on his hands helping himself to other people's port which was considered really good form! Then it was the turn of our own regiments march. Everyone stood up and banged the table loudly as the band marched around the dining hall playing. Glasses shook and tumbled and many a long dress was ruined by spilt port. Music over we all sat down again and waited expectantly for the RSM to leave the dining room but oh no............not yet.................. thank the waiters, most of whom were by now so pissed they did not know who was being thanked, then thank the chefs who were, as always, impressive. I have never had a meal that has bettered those meals served up on those nights and then, the RSM moved! Stampede to the toilets. Wives pushed out of the way! Relief!

The entertainment would then start and the bar reopen. Considering it was nearly midnight by this time the bar became very busy. Everyone was talking. Wives were talking about husbands and husbands were almost without exception, talking about their job, talking shop. Wives grabbed husbands and dragged them onto the dance floor. If their husband was incapable they grabbed someone else's husband or a single SNCO to dance with. Dancing was good! Made you sweat which created room for more booze!

Coaches home at one o'clock. Ooops! Was that the coach? Have to stay until the next one won't we. No longer on a promise!

TROOP SERGEANT AND THE GULF

Lt Col (Retd) John Walker.

Whilst I was promoted to Sergeant in March '86, I was immediately posted to the Driving and Maintenance (D&M) School at Bovington for 2 ½ years and then spent some time with the Regiment teaching D&M to Phase 2 students at Catterick. As a result, the period covered here runs from the Regiment's arrival in Fallingbostel to shortly after the first Gulf War at which point I was promoted to Staff Sergeant. Please forgive what are likely to be a large number of chronological and factual errors during what will be a seriously disjointed account. I have simply cherry picked events that still remain as memories.

Obviously, much of what follows covers the deployment to the Gulf War. Whilst my account includes a number of episodes I considered to be funny at the time, I am extremely conscious that a number of my friends and colleagues experienced events that negatively and profoundly affected them and I therefore stress that it is not my intent to either glorify the war or to make light of it in any way.

Having arrived in Fallingbostel, taken over the tanks, and the roughly seven billion individual items associated with them, we began a series of troop level teach-ins and low level training exercises. The training was designed to re-acquaint us older individuals with the basics of living on our tanks and to introduce these delights to our newbies. Following these quite pleasant and informal activities, we moved on to tactical movement and low level war fighting tactics which might have been equally enjoyable had they not highlighted significant deficiencies in our abilities to read maps, use the communications systems properly, stay awake at critical points in the battle, carry out important servicing tasks and generally remember anything that, a couple of years previously, would have been second nature. Embarrassment is a great motivator; we learned rapidly and effectively.

During one of our numerous jaunts to Soltau Training Area, we were joined by Cornet Henry Camilleri. Henry was 'given' to

Corporal Dave Ronayne as an extra crewman on Callsign 22 and given strict instructions on what not to do. As a newly commissioned Officer, Henry was naturally considered fair game by the Troop. During a lull in the fighting, we found ourselves close to Rheinsehlen Camp with a 'No move before' time of a couple of hours away. The Troop, less Henry, congregated on the turret of 21 (all tanks had their own callsigns) to discuss the upcoming activities. We suddenly realised that Henry had gone to sleep on top of the loaders basket of 22, with one leg dangling through the side bars of the basket, and he was very slowly sliding sideways. A fall would have resulted in his being suspended upside down and urgent bets were now being taken on the eventual outcome and potential injury levels. James and I looked at each other and slowly but quite deliberately turned away and began serious discussions on something or other. At the last safe moment, Henry awoke. He looked over to see the entire troop staring at him in a state of abject disappointment. I'm not convinced he ever knew what that was all about....until he reads this of course.

In the summer of 1990, I decided to raise my regimental profile by attending an All Arms Advanced Drill Instructor course at the Guards Depot, Pirbright. I acquired two pairs of drill boots and an extra No2 Dress uniform. Thinking myself thoroughly prepared, I set off for the UK. On arrival at the School, I was greeted like a long lost brother by Colour Sergeant Jim Rayner, shown my room and invited to the Mess for a drink. Following a pleasant evening, I returned to my room and prepared my kit for the following morning. I had breakfast, and on my way back to the room I bumped into Jim Raynor in the corridor. "Morning Jim", I said cheerfully. This resulted in the first of many trips to the Guardroom, there to be drilled mercilessly by the Duty Instructor for 10 minutes for incorrectly addressing a Drill Instructor. On occasions, my own naivety astounds even me! I was sent to the tailors to have my cavalry sacking turned into a No2 Dress just at the time when the course photo was taken so I was the only one incorrectly dressed and once again I attended the Guardroom.

During the next 6 weeks, my fellow students and I saw our seemingly immaculate kit launched across rooms and out of windows. We delivered drill lessons with our heads thrust inside the hedge that ran around the outside of the Parade Square, consumed vast quantities of port purchased, by ourselves, as punishment for minor infringements of Mess etiquette such as blinking, failing to stand when the instructors favourite song came on the sound system, not being able to deliver a lesson effectively at 0400hrs etc etc. Those, like me, who took it all in the right spirit thoroughly enjoyed the experience. Those that didn't, didn't.

I returned to Fallingbostel in time for a regimental exercise and troop tests. During the exercise I developed conjunctivitis in both eyes and had to spend a night in Rheinsehlen camp. I was given some gunk to put in my eyes that prevented me from seeing anything for a couple of hours at a time. I was sat on my bed wearing nothing but underpants when the door opened and someone stomped in. I stood and helplessly gazed around trying to focus and identify the visitor. When I heard the very familiar and terrifying voice of the Commanding Officer, Lt Col Arthur Denaro, enquiring as to why we were there and what we thought we were doing, I stopped breathing and came very close to giving birth to a quantity of kittens. Happily, and just as Armageddon was about to be triggered, he realised I was temporarily blind and I was reprieved.

I should add, at this point, that the arrival of Lt Col Denaro heralded a monumental culture change across the Regiment. We stopped drinking alcohol on exercise. Those readers not acquainted with the British Army during the Cold War years might find this a trivial point; those who are more knowledgeable will experience a sharp intake of breath.

Once the training was out of the way, a JNCO Cadre was run. The course qualified senior Troopers for promotion to Lance Corporal and provided individuals with their moment to shine amongst their peers. In the QRIH, the individual identified as the best student was automatically promoted so the course was taken seriously. As the most newly qualified and Pirbright trained Drill Instructor, I was appointed Drill Sergeant under Major Hugh Pierson and we set about preparing the course. I was fortunate to have Terry Jonas as my Cpl and was really looking forward to it. At this point, the rumours relating to a desert deployment were rife.

I had just returned from preparing a route for an orienteering event when Major Pierson informed me that the Regiment was to deploy to the Gulf, that the Cadre was cancelled and that we were to send all students back to their Squadrons immediately. And so it began.

Once 7 Armoured Brigade was given the go ahead for the deployment, daily activity became frenetic in the extreme. We reported for work at around 0600hrs and began every day with fitness training followed by a round robin of training sessions covering Nuclear, Biological and Chemical warfare (NBC), first aid, vehicle recognition, health and hygiene, small arms, interspersed with writing wills, being jabbed with numerous concoctions of chemicals, dental checks and country briefings etc. The NBC training was provided by a team from the Queen's Own Hussars, headed up by Sgt (Latterly RSM and LE Lt Col QRH) Tom Hamilton. Tom continues to this day to bemoan the fact that the dubious literature he placed in the Gas Chamber, to take our minds off the impending horror of being gassed, was all stolen by my Troop; clearly an erroneous slander on his part and no court would ever convict us. Our fitness training was taken care of by WO2 (SSM) Nigel Briggs. We had to be fit, we were going to war, and Nigel got us fit in such a way that we hardly noticed; it was hard work, but he didn't try to kill us on day one. He worked us up to a good level over a reasonable period until we were running fitness tests in our NBC suits!

I was the Troop Sergeant of 2nd Troop, B Squadron of the Irish Hussars, commanded by Major David Swann and with Captain Johnny Ormorod as the Squadron Second in Command. David's calm, methodical and diplomatic leadership was countered perfectly by Johnny's clear and sometimes quite angry intent to get everything done as quickly as possible. Johnny does not suffer fools gladly and on a number of occasions I was clearly being a fool and fell foul of his sharp tongue. I'm sure I was not the only one, but I'm equally sure it felt like it at the time. I like to tell myself that I treated these as learning events and that I was grateful for the 'education'.

The majority of the B Squadron personalities had been in the Squadron when I joined it and we had been troopers together. We knew each other well and got on well as a group. In addition, we all had a very similar sense of humour; some might call it dark. Mistakes were inevitably met with torrents of friendly but ruthless verbal abuse.

In amongst all of this, we learnt that we would be provided with tanks from other regiments (later builds than ours) and that we would need to prepare them for deployment. We de-kitted our tanks and parked them on the edge of the Tank Park. The Irish Hussars always put enormous effort into handing over equipment to other units in good order and having spent our careers carefully accounting for every nut and bolt, it came as a major culture shock to be told that if we found anything unserviceable on one of the new tanks, we should simply replace it with a serviceable item from one of the old ones. I should have felt sorry for the donors of the new tanks, but we simply didn't have time, we just left the unserviceable items loose in the turrets...someone else's problem. Life was very strange for us during those days, it was almost as if all the rules we had lived by previously were suddenly dropped.

We had to confirm the tanks combat serviceability by firing on the ranges at Hohne. Normally, this would have involved hours of preparing ammunition, firing points, painting the tanks followed by all the associated cleaning up afterwards. For this range period, we simply turned up, fired our allotted rounds and drove back to camp while all the donkey work was done for us by the Queen's Own Hussars, bless them. It was clear that a vast number of people were working extremely hard to help us get ready for deployment. This was getting serious!

In late September, all the vehicles had departed for the Gulf and about two weeks later we flew out.

We had left Fallingbostel on a very fresh and early autumnal morning, so the heat of Saudi literally took our breath away. From the airport, we were transported to the port of Al Jubayl and accommodated in gigantic warehouses. We slept on camp beds in as little clothing as we could while maintaining some semblance of propriety; the Medical Officer (MO) was a female and shared our lavish accommodation. Naturally, we had to acclimatise to the heat and, obviously, we adopted the Irish Hussar method which was to run around the port in the blazing heat until we got used to it

(I'm writing this, so it must have worked although it didn't feel like it at the time. We all thought it was insanity). The Engineers had erected showers adjacent to each warehouse and these were almost permanently in use as we moved between PT, NBC training, weapon training and briefings. We were, at the time, attached to a United States Marine Corps division and there was much swapping of regimental paraphernalia for American camp cots and other such luxuries. Down time was spent topping up the sun tan, legally and illegally procuring useful items of equipment and fishing for very dubious fish from the dockside. Even our most experienced fishermen could not recognise some of the monstrosities dragged screaming out of those waters.

At some point, we were directed to start taking some tablets. Much has been said about the various drugs we were directed to take and that we were injected with. There was equal concern over the 'new' ammunition we used on the tanks. Aside from a greenish glow that emanates from my fifteen toes at around 0624 each morning, I do not believe I have suffered any lasting side effects.

On the 25th of October, Balaklava Day, the vast majority of the Regiment were transported to a beach where we ate, drank (no alcohol), swam in the sea, took part in an inter Squadron bed race and generally fooled around. When we got back to the port, my skin suddenly began to itch. The itching spread over my entire body and almost drove me crazy. On and off, I spent around seven hours in the shower; the only thing that would stop the madness. At around six the next morning, I conceded defeat and made the decision to approach the MO. I wandered over to her bed space and as I approached, I suddenly became aware that the itching had stopped...just like that and never to return...bizarre.

I had cause to seek medical attention twice during the deployment. I grew some extremely unsightly and uncomfortable lumps in my armpits which I naturally took to be some sort of terminal middle east specific disease, but which turned out to be infected sweat glands (probably brought on by seven hours in the shower). Secondly, I had some sort of back spasm which was cured by an army Physical Training Corps physiotherapist who, in a previous life had clearly held the rank of SS Obersturmbannfuhrer, thumping my back until I, and my back, surrendered. I thankfully remained in rude health from then on.

The temperatures in the port were extreme. The heat, together with humidity of around 90% made life very uncomfortable. Consequently, any down time when we could revert to shorts and flip flops was considered precious. We were therefore less than impressed when we were told to put on full uniform one evening as an American actor, known for his rather slapstick comedies, would be walking around and we should give the right impression (?!). As he passed through, the celebrity asked an Hussar, "How y'a doing?" The response from the seriously unhappy individual was along the lines of "How the f*** do you think I'm doing?" Years of acting training failed miserably to kick in and the esteemed visitor merely mumbled and walked on.

About four days later, and following a desert upgrade to our vehicles, we escaped the humidity of the port and deployed into the desert on our tanks...hurrah. Living on a tank in the desert is worlds away from living on a tank on Soltau training area. There are no scorpions on Soltau, there are many in the desert and they vary in size, colour and strength of venom. There are also many, many insects, most of which appeared to have been specially bred to identify and occupy gaps in the human skin. We were also introduced to the 'stand to' which involved occupying crew positions and deploying sentries from some 15 minutes before dawn and dusk until some 15 minutes after. This was highly successful as we stood to at first and last light every day we were deployed on our vehicles and we were never once attacked at either dawn or dusk!

At this early time, we were sleeping on issued camp beds which are uncomfortable and way too close to the ground for our liking. I awoke one morning to find my loader, Paul Rudd, shouting for me. Turns out he had sat up on his camp bed and lifted his Bergen to be confronted by a large and almost fluorescent green scorpion with murder in its eyes. Quite why Paul thought I was any better qualified to deal with this than he was, I simply do not know. Given that the centre of our camp beds almost touched the floor, this did not bode well for our future health and it was not long before our crew entrepreneur, Adrian Black, acquired some camp cots for us. I have never been any good at acquiring stuff, I just can't approach someone and wheel and deal, it's not in my DNA. Adrian, however, was seriously good at it and would beg, steal or borrow (permanently) anything and everything to make life easier.

The desert we inhabited was not the romantic desert from the movies with towering dunes and noble Arabs on white chargers strutting their stuff. This desert was a vast flat expanse of dirty grey brown sand, littered with copious amounts of very dubious 'stuff' and with the odd hill breaking up the horizon. Our maps might as well have been sheets of sandpaper. Early on, there was plenty of ambient light during the night. Later, however, when the weather turned for the worse, I had my first experience of being outside but literally unable to see my hand in front of my face. Radio stags were a necessary pain and being unable to use artificial light when moving from the ground to the turret and back again by feel alone was incredibly difficult.

Whenever we stopped we put up camouflage nets and latterly, we were issued with rolls of Chemical Agent Resistant Material (CARM – at least I think that is what it was called) which we used to cover sleeping areas. Tanks are not smooth; they are covered in 'hooks' that cam nets will catch on at every possible opportunity. After a relatively short period however, we could cam up and de-cam a tank in record time and without particularly thinking about it. I often wondered why we didn't develop those skills to the same extent on exercise.

Carrying out your ablutions in the desert can also be a trifle strange and is nothing like taking a "shovel recce" on exercise in Germany. Soltau does not have large flying beetles that sound like Chinook helicopters that swoop down and roll away all evidence of your activities before you have had time to dig a hole. That took some getting used to!

Exchange visits were arranged between the Regiment and one of the USMC tank battalions and I was lucky enough to spend a night with the Marines. I have to say that their tanks were positively prehistoric, and they knew it. They firmly believed they were the poor relations to the US Army armoured units which was a bit sad. I found them to be extremely professional and proud of their unit and heritage. While we waited for our transport, I stood next to a bonfire and was engaged in conversation by a large black gentleman. He shook me by the hand and introduced himself as Chuck (if my memory serves me correctly). I introduced myself as John and we had a good chat during which I was very complimentary about the men, but less flattering when it came to the tanks. Shortly after, **Colonel** Chuck (Commander, 3 Tank Battalion, USMC) was called away by one of his Officers and I thanked God, Allah and anyone else I could think of that: a) none of our own Officers had been within earshot and b) Col Chuck had a sense of humour.

My Squadron conducted a long move one day during which James Rainbird's tank broke down. He directed me to carry on with Dave Ronayne on the expectation that the REME would recover him shortly. On arrival at our destination, we occupied a squadron position, put up our camouflage nets and began to enjoy a brief period of relaxation. Almost immediately, the Squadron Leader appeared and informed me that no REME recovery assets were available and that I would have to go and tow James back using my tank. I knew James was almost exactly 20 Km South of our location, so I took a compass bearing, pointed the gun barrel along that bearing and told Junior Blackman, my driver, to follow the barrel and to stop when he had driven for 10 Km. The turret on a tank is stabilised so that the barrel will remain pointing at a target regardless of what the hull is doing below it. After 10Km, Junior stopped, and I jumped off the tank to confirm the bearing. I will admit to some consternation when I discovered we were 90 degrees off course; so much for stabilisation! I turned the tank through 180 degrees and repeated the process and we drove straight to the right location. So, stabilisation worked badly, but at least it worked consistently badly. We hooked up the dead tank and towed it back to the Squadron (in a relatively straight line this time).

By the time we arrived, I was aware that towing the dead tank across 20Km of sand had had a detrimental effect on my own vehicle. I reported the fact to the Squadron Headquarters and we took the tank to the REME for repairs. So began a saga of woe. The strain placed on my engine had caused a seal to blow and a resulting oil leak. The leak was repaired, and I returned to my location. Shortly after, my troop was picked up by tank transporter and moved to another location to take part in a comparison trial with a troop from the Scots DG. Our tanks were configured differently and the powers that be wanted to know how each would perform. We carried out some servicing tasks and tests and then drove around a circuit. About halfway round the circuit, my engine died and the electronics system went crazy; it was like a disco in the turret. We also had a fire in the back decks which we extinguished and waited for recovery.

Eventually we were moved to the A1 Echelon where we awaited the necessary spares. After some of the work was done, we were able to move the tank but could not use some of the more critical services such as the NBC equipment and the main armament and so we remained with the Echelon (the regimental logistic organisation). When the A2 echelon was required to move, I was asked to drive one of the 4 Tonne trucks due to their lack of qualified drivers. When we arrived at the new location, I waited for Callsign 21 to arrive. Instead, I was informed that my crew had decided to drive straight through a sabkha (dried up lake) and was somewhat stuck. I was given a lift to their location and found I could walk straight on to the back decks without climbing the 5-6 feet normally required; a good indication of how deep my tank had sunk. It took the Recovery Mechanics quite some time to extract the tank and my crew quite some time to get over it. Around this time, we were given the opportunity to go on a shower run. While we were away, some of our comrades in arms relieved us of our camp cots which we had stupidly left out. This 'military recycling' was a catastrophe and Adrian had to be deployed for replacements.

Just when it seemed like we might get back to the battle, we had another fire and the situation for us became even worse. We were moved to a deployed Repair Group belonging to 7 Armoured Workshops. A Repair Group (RG) is a large organisation and I was not convinced it had deployed into the field...ever. There appeared to be much flapping around and shouting. I have to say we were not treated well. We were used as guards during the night, put on fatigues during the day and basically shunned the rest of the time. After a while, we were moved back to the port, although I'm not sure if the whole RG was moved or just us. I'm pretty sure my mind has taken the whole experience of being 'looked after' by an RG and simply wiped it from my memory.

Our first visit to a shop was shortly after our arrival back in port with the RG. We had come straight from the desert and we, and our clothes, were filthy in the extreme. Paul Rudd and I were stood in a queue and I became aware that our condition was clearly upsetting some of the shiny and immaculately dressed rear echelon bunnies queuing with us. As the smoke began to emanate from Paul's ears I engaged him in some trivial conversation in the hope that it would prevent him from laying waste to all those around us. It must have worked because I don't recall a Court Martial!

While we waited in the port for the repair decision, we took the opportunity to de-kit the vehicle and clean and service all the appropriate components and systems. We also took the opportunity to visit the NAAFI shop and American PX etc. I should also say that anything that looked like it might make life on a tank more comfortable was duly stolen and stashed away safely. During this time, our own REME used my tank as a source for any spares that were not immediately available. They also informed me that the initial repair had been carried out incorrectly resulting in a fuel pipe splitting and squirting fuel into the electrical generator; hence the fire and disco! My crew and I were not happy bunnies. We were away from the Squadron because of a botched repair, and our tank was becoming more and more skeletal by the day. Whenever any friendly faces passed our way, I implored them to pass on our tale of woe to the chain of command in the hope that someone might actually notice we were no longer in the desert and send a rescue team.

Eventually, we were offered our choice of 2 replacement tanks; I should have been suspicious from the outset. One was brand new and absolutely immaculate; the other was functional but dirty and tired. No contest I hear you say. That was my reaction until I was told that the new tank had been painted with a special paint that had a bit of a side effect; it gave off cyanide fumes when heated. "Did that include being heated by something like, say, an enemy round hitting the tank?" I asked, knowing exactly what the answer would be. "Yes" came the response and we immediately began transferring our equipment to the old bucket in the corner. By this time, we had been stuck in the workshops, in a variety of locations, for something like seven weeks so we were very glad to be back in the desert; it didn't matter that our mode of transport was a tank slightly less dependable and even less aesthetically pleasing than a Morris Marina. We just had to get out of there!

When we returned to the Squadron, we were welcomed back by our 2nd troop lads and by 1st troop, Sgt Andy Vick and his boys. We were then thoroughly abused by 3rd troop's Sgt Pete Connor and Cpl Dave Garrigan. It was a point of pride that any opportunity whatsoever to take the micky out of a comrade was immediately seized upon. It mattered not a jot that our prolonged absence was not our fault, we were ruthlessly set upon regardless. We expected nothing else and were extremely glad to be back.

We were introduced to some amazing new technology in the desert. Many of our moves took place in total darkness and identifying the tank in front, when there were many tanks moving, was very difficult. We were therefore directed to cut off the lids from tins in our ration packs and attach them to the extra fuel tanks on the rear of the vehicles in a particular pattern. When using the thermal imaging equipment, the metal disks showed up and allowed us to identify and maintain sight of the tank in front. Troop Leaders were issued with Trimble Global Positioning Systems (GPS) so that at least 1 tank commander in each troop knew his location. Sadly, in those days, there were significantly less satellites than there are now so there were long periods when the GPS couldn't function.

We were into a cycle of moving between the desert, Camp 4 in Al Jubayl and St Patricks Camp. St Patrick's Camp had been established in the desert to provide a brief respite from living on the tanks and self catering etc. Light and noise discipline was still followed at nights and cam nets were put up. Camp 4 was a hutted camp in the port where we were completely non-tactical and could wander around in shorts. The couple of days in Camp 4 provided an opportunity to phone home which was marvellous and extremely welcome. Equally welcome was the burger bar and the shops that had sprung up. On one visit, Andy Vick (1st Tp Sgt) and I hired a car and went down the coast to Al Khobar to do some pre Christmas shopping. The population appeared happy and carefree. I made the mistake of showing an interest in a particularly fine (and expensive) camera in one shop and was followed and harassed by the shopkeeper for quite some time and distance. Clearly, he thought rabid persistence was valid retail methodology.

Bahrain was also a short drive from Al Jubayl, but for reasons known only to the hierarchy (probably the availability of alcohol which was forbidden in Saudi), we were strictly forbidden from going there. This was seen as a challenge, probably by a number of Hussars, but definitely by two members of my crew. Unfortunately, one of their friends from a different squadron failed to return with them and their crime went public much to the consternation of their bank managers. We were, of course, delighted to learn that the RAF were living in 5* hotels in Bahrain!

I don't think I ever saw SSM Nigel Briggs down in the dumps in all the time we were out there. He was, and is, one of the most upbeat men I have ever known and we, his troop Sergeants, counted ourselves lucky to have him as our SSM. Many readers will have seen the photographs of the exploding Centurion armoured vehicles. Folklore has it that the vehicles were bombed up and fully fuelled and that the crews had been wiping down the (hot) back decks with petrol which had led to the subsequent fire and explosions. I witnessed the event from the top of my tank and, I have to say, it was mightily impressive even from a couple of kilometres away. Nigel was significantly closer and caught some of the blast as he sprinted away. When he returned to us, he immediately and proudly dropped his coveralls to show us the blanket bruising covering his back and legs. Whilst it must have been painful, Nigel showed pretty much everyone, whether they wanted to see or not, and grinned happily throughout the ordeal.

Christmas was spent with the Regiment centred on St Patrick's Camp. The chefs served up an amazing Christmas dinner ably assisted by General Sir Peter de la Billiere (the British Commander in the field), which was a bit of a shock. In the evening, there was a regimental review which provided an opportunity for some comedy for the many at the expense of those few who bore the brunt.

Battlefield discipline in the desert was, quite rightly, rigidly enforced. Stories of individuals being dealt with severely for what might have been classed as minor infractions were rife. During a particularly wet period, one of our crew shelters collapsed and soaked much of the occupant's clothing and equipment. Naturally, we all pulled together and, with the help of some hot engines, went about drying everything. The running of the engines and the movement of personnel attracted the attention of the Commanding Officer who came over to see what was going on. No announcement, he simply appeared by my left shoulder and quietly enquired as to what was happening. More kittens! I explained the situation and, to my surprise, did not have to pack my kit and move to a new appointment as Camp 4 road sweeper for the duration.

Our biggest luxuries by far were the letters and parcels from home. In the desert we had little or no access to 'goodies' and the arrival of a parcel was a major event. My far better other half, Mags, sent me pistachio nuts, chocolate, Du Maurier cigarettes and other bits that really brightened the gloom. Her letters were cheerful and most of my early morning radio stags were spent writing replies. We had to be careful what we wrote in order to maintain operational security, even though we had journalists with us who reported, equally carefully, on what we were doing.

We fired the tanks on Jerboa Range, that had been set up in the desert. As we moved forwards, I expressed disgust at the sight of an apparently dead and bloated camel lying some 20 yards to our left. As we fired the main armament, the 'dead' camel gave birth at high velocity, stood up and began to tend to its new born calf. You don't get that on Soltau!

As G Day loomed ever closer, we practiced moving through the breaches in the Iraqi defences; berms, minefields, wire and ditches etc. Friendly and enemy forces were marked as blue and red on maps and it sometimes appeared that we would be moving into a sea of red when we crossed over. Right up until G Day, the indication was that we would meet fierce resistance.

When the air war began, we watched the aircraft flying over on their way to deliver some messages to the Iraqi positions. I would not have liked to have been in those positions. The deliveries were precise and highly technical, targeting control and communication centres, airfields and the like; all designed to destroy the Iraqi capability and morale.

In our squadron areas, we had pits dug for the disposal of rubbish. The SSM called the vehicle commanders over for a brief one morning and stood with his back to one such pit, thankfully an empty one. At this stage I should point out that Nigel was not one to allow a trivial thing like hair loss spoil his body beautiful Physical Training Instructor image and sported a comb-over that we firmly believed was a sentient being. During the brief, he stepped back and promptly disappeared, followed some time later by his comb-over. There was a mighty thump as he landed flat on his back in the bottom of the trench. Awkward moment of silence followed by Nigel rebounding off the floor and landing in a pose that a 14 year old Russian gymnast would have been extremely proud of and a shout of "Ta Daaa". The awkward moment continued for several more moments (he was the SSM after all) until suddenly we were all afflicted with a serious dose of almost terminal laughter. I, for one, thought I was going to die and I'm fairly sure Dave Garrigan had a hernia.

G Day arrived, and the time finally came for us to move through the Iraqi defences. Given the anticipated resistance, I fully expected this to be the scariest thing I would ever do, command a tank in war. To my surprise, my reaction was one of excitement and a real desire to get on with the job. At the end of the first day, my bucket of a tank died and I was given a new power pack. Sadly, there were no air new cleaner elements available, so we had to use the existing heavily constricted element. When we moved off, we could only manage a few miles per hour and soon found ourselves having to stop and clean out the air cleaner on a very regular basis. This meant moving alone, in daylight, during the ground war, a potentially scary situation. At one point, a British Major approached on foot and asked us to provide flank protection for the Brigade Headquarters as it moved forward (faster than us). Eventually, we caught the Squadron up and took up our position.

The ground offensive, and the war, was over before we knew it and I will not dwell on it; there are many published accounts already.

Once a cease fire was announced, we moved into holding positions and awaited orders. Sadaam Hussein's forces had destroyed many of the oil wells as part of his scorched earth policy and the sky was black with the smoke of burning oil. We were briefed to carry out stringent checks on our areas for unexploded bombs, anti-personnel mines and other dangers. Once we had cleared and marked out safe areas and there was no further threat, we were allowed to go non-tactical.

That evening I sat in my turret and wrote what I hoped would be my final letter from the desert to Mags. As I climbed out, I saw a bonfire with a number of individuals sitting around it. I wandered over and came across Nigel Briggs and others passing round what appeared to be a bottle of shampoo. Nigel was clearly enjoying the contents so when I was offered the bottle I took a hefty swig. It was indeed shampoo that had been very slightly contaminated with Whisky. I would dearly like to say that I enjoyed partaking of this forbidden delicacy, but I would be lying through my teeth, it was foul! It was probably the only item of contraband that made it through the mail screening process, after all, who would be mad enough to put Whisky in a shampoo bottle?

We were able to conduct a number of battlefield tours during this period and, as responsible members of the Armed Forces, we picked up everything and anything that even vaguely looked like a trophy. During these tours, it became clear that the Iraqi forces had bugged out very quickly without taking much with them, and that they had very little in the way of personal or military equipment or resources in the first place. We were flown in a Sea King over the area and saw the carnage inflicted upon the enemy forces along the Basra road. Truly, truly awful. We also saw the effect that the smart bombs and missiles used by the Americans had on aircraft hangars and other installations. The scale of the operation was also brought home to us when we saw, from the air, the number and size of the abandoned enemy positions.

Once the order was given to move the Regiment back to Germany, we moved very quickly through a de-kitting process. All ammunition and other items of equipment were removed from the tanks and we moved them to a holding area. I have mentioned before that a number of individuals were removed from post for a variety of transgressions. When told to report immediately to the CO, I naturally assumed that my apparent inability to keep my tank moving for more than twelve minutes at a time had finally been noticed and that my next posting would be rapid and would probably involve a gulag somewhere very cold and remote. Thankfully, that wasn't the case and whilst a move was imminent, my immediate future was reasonably secure.

Despite the unfortunate sequence of events that caused my crew and I to be away from the Squadron for prolonged periods, we were there at the beginning of the ground offensive and we managed to get the bucket to the right place, albeit slowly, for all of the important bits. I was immensely proud to be an Irish Hussar. We did what had to be done and we did it professionally. We were extremely lucky that we had exactly the right people in the right command appointments at exactly the right time.

In what seemed like no time at all, we were on board a 747 bound for Germany. We were allowed 2 cans of beer (hah, like that was going to happen!) and allowed to smoke on the plane. The pilot said some nice things over the tannoy and some of the guys swapped uniforms with the cabin staff. All in all, one of the least boring flights I have experienced.

When we arrived in Fallingbostel, the QRIH Pipes and Drums led the coaches into camp and on to the parade square where our families were waiting. The raw emotion on the coach as we pulled up was palpable and I am not the slightest bit embarrassed to say that I cried like a two year old when Mags, Melissa and Robert came running up to me.

After a period of leave during which the family and I drove the length and breadth of UK to catch up with everyone, we began the process of checking the vehicles and equipment in order to establish what had dropped off, been chucked away, lost, used up or pinched during our time in the desert. The list was long, and the process was painful but very necessary. The move to becoming a unit destined for warfighting operations had been a rapid and exciting one. The move back to peacetime regulations and accounting was quite the opposite.

Shortly after this, I handed the Troop over to Dave Ronayne, left B Squadron and tanks behind for the last time and moved into the voodoo infested world of logistics. My brief but eventful tenure as a troop Sgt, some 26 years ago, was over.

THE SENIOR MAN

Lt.Col Loopy Kennard, CO, 4TH QOHUSSARS. I never forgot the answer he gave the Brigadier on the Tank Bridge over the Weser when asked "Who is the senior Man here?"

"You are Brigadier!" Loopy replied.

TEA BAGS AND BELTS

It used to be the norm that those more challenged by a life serving on tanks would find their way into the stores, either in Headquarter Squadron or in a sabre squadron stores. One such young man I shall call Ginge. Ginge was posted into HQ Squadron SQMS stores where he faced a number of challenges. On his arrival, he was being issued with his "G10" (large pack and pouches, sleeping bag and much more including the old webbed belt). The SQMS told him to go and get a belt from the cellar where they were stored and then hurry back so he could be issued the rest of the stuff. After about half an hour a frustrated SQMS went down to the cellar to see what Ginge was up to. Ginge stood in the centre of the room. On his right was a large box that had contained hundreds of webbed belts. On his left were the belts. "What the F...are you doing?" asked the SQMS. "I can't get one to fit." Was the reply. Webbed belts are one size and adjustable. What he had done in basic training no one knows!

Shortly after this incident the Regiment deployed to Soltau. Ginge was kept out of the way and conducted menial tasks. He was instructed to go and make a brew. The SQMS took one sip and spat his tea out. It was full of tea leaves. Ginge had cut the tea bags open and then tipped the contents into the kettle. What he had done whilst growing up at home no one knows either!

AMALGAMATION

Mergers between regiments have been going on for a very long time. It is how the Queens Own Hussars and The Queen's Royal Irish Hussars came into being. What is important is how an amalgamation is managed and the realisation that the new Regiment is the embodiment of both the old regiments and must be supported as vigorously by Old Comrades as they supported their own regiments in the past. Serving soldiers deserve nothing less.

The QOH and QRIH had a pretty long lead in time to amalgamation, long enough to do a joint tour in Cyprus and for the various messes to get together on social nights. Committees had some time to discuss what traditions and clothing would stay and what would go. You can never please everybody. Some complained about green jumpers and others complained about mess dress but by most standards amalgamation went well. There was not the angst that had reputedly occurred in other amalgamations of cavalry regiments.

The first RSM, WO1 Brian Nicholl, was excellent in ensuring the Sergeants mess did not become factional. The CO, Andrew Bellamy ensured that members of both former regiments worked as a team and gelled as quickly as possible. An even split between QOH and QRIH in tanks crews and squadrons was one method. I have to say that at times I thought he was completely potty (particularly when he said we were about to go to war with Russia on the regiments return from ranges!) as I had not seen the big picture and only subsequently realised how cleverly he had moulded the team. The normal run of things settled the Regiment. Ranges, exercises and a BATUS that was a huge success (but saw a tragic accident involving our Infantry from 1 Devon and Dorsets) ensured that armoured skills were honed. Suffice to say that we gelled quickly and that the new Queens Royal Hussars gained a reputation on its way to match that of both former regiments very quickly. One thing was still to be achieved, the presentation of a Guidon to the Queens Royal Hussars but a part of Europe called the Balkans delayed proceedings.

A year or so after the amalgamation I found out there had been at least one fight on the day of amalgamation. John Nutt and Andy Burnett were sharing a joke or two over a pint in the mess when they began talking of amalgamation. Nutty told of how there had been a fight in one of the bars and of how some low life had pulled his (Nutty's) jacket over his head and then continued to punch him. Andy smiled and owned up! The spirit of Hussars does not change.

PRESENTATION OF THE GUIDON TO THE QUEEN'S ROYAL HUSSARS

Brigadier Nick Smith

When considering what to write on the Guidon Parade Weekend, my initial thoughts were that it should be quite a straightforward task. Many memories came flooding back and the areas that should be addressed seemed to be fairly obvious. However, as I suspect anyone who has sought to delve into their memory and recall the events of 20 years earlier has found, recollection of the detail proves to be more challenging than the happy recollection of certain snapshots replayed whenever the topic has come up in the intervening years. So I have found and when consulting others I have also found that their memories, or at least the limitations of them, seem little different from my own. I therefore apologise in advance to those who read this and find themselves with a different recollection of events. I can only say that if my memory is at fault it is unintentional. It was a great three days and there is no need to be revisionist. I will happily debate what reality was over a pint.

Well before I assumed command I knew I was going to have the privilege of having the Regiment's new Guidon presented during my tenure; there was no way that it was going to slip past another Commanding Officer. I was a Squadron Leader and then Second in Command under Andrew Bellamy and took no convincing then that the presentation of the new Guidon should not be rushed and should await the Regiment's return to Catterick. It seemed eminently sensible, at that time, and Nigel Beer after all would relish the opportunity, would he not? As it happened Nigel's tour was dominated by Bosnia and the arms plot move so there was no time to fit it in. So it was, somewhat ironically, that I found myself holding the baby and initially was not sure how to view that. We are all captives of our experiences and the most relevant experience that I had was of The Queen's Own Hussars Tercentenary Parade and celebrations. I advisedly say parade and celebrations as the Regiment made a huge effort to mark the anniversary appropriately.

117

The event was spread over three days and involved an array of activities and spectacles, to make it an appropriately memorable occasion for all who attended and much else was also done, through the production of books and the commissioning of suitable memorabilia, to mark the event. The Tercentenary was, therefore, in my mind complex and somewhat daunting in scale. Having had a chance to reflect I could, however, see that there was no need to seek to replicate the Tercentenary. Rather we needed to work out what was right and appropriate for this particular event and, although drawing on the experience of previous events, should avoid being hostage to them. The start point was the date. On looking at the diary the only possible window was between BATUS in November of 1996 and the Northern Ireland tour at the end of 1997. The majority of the Regiment was to deploy to Armagh at the beginning of October 1997 but training began in mid June. With my sharpest memory of the Tercentenary Parade being the torrential rain that fell as stair rods through much of it and which, despite the admirable resolve of all involved, did detract from the day it seemed sensible to at least plan on a day when the weather was most likely to be kind, accepting that it was Yorkshire. This led us to going for Friday 13 June. There was no scope to be superstitious; we could not leave it any later, with the hierarchy departing on the Sunday for Folkstone, for the Northern Ireland Commanders' Cadre. When it came to planning it was, as ever, finding the capacity to do the detailed planning and preparation for the day which was critical and in this we were helped by the nature of the Northern Ireland tour which involved only three squadron headquarters and RHQ, although it deployed, did not have an operational role. This gave us the head room to be able to plan and organise the event. Andrew Cuthbert was the Squadron Leader departing and not deploying on the tour and was, therefore, self selecting as the project officer for the Guidon parade. He of course welcomed the "honour" and in his own inimitable style set about ensuring that the day was the best that could be organised.

Cuthy was supported by a small Guidon Office team. Alex Bather, who had recovered from his close encounter with a tank barrel in BATUS, moved in, the Parade being his last act before leaving, and "Nipper" Walker, newly commissioned, brought his considerable talents. The core team could only deliver the event if we had the right people to address all of the essential elements and in this I found myself in an extremely fortunate position. In any team you anticipate having to carry someone or at least make allowances for some limitations, but I found myself with an exceptional cast. As ever the Quartermaster was key. When he is good so many issues seem to lead back to his desk, even when they probably should not. In Paul Hodgson I had one of the best and his sure touch ensured that the myriad of administrative and logistical aspects were identified early on and effective solutions found. He was well supported, and I should mention in particular WO2 Jenkinson, our Master Chef, who in those bygone days when Army chefs were present in strength, enabled us to plan and to provide exactly the right fare for the many meals that were needed. Keith Deakin's Headquarters Squadron and all its departments stepped up to the mark without fuss, ensuring that what needed to be done was done and done well. Having lost the Band just after amalgamation the Band that was going to support us was going to be critical, not least because of the need to combine with our own Pipes and Drums. I was well aware that there were differing attitudes towards pipe bands and if we were going to have the music that we wanted and to be able to stamp the style we wished to achieve on the occasion it was essential that we had a band that saw the Pipes and Drums as an asset and not something to have to accommodate. The logical choice was, of course, the recently formed Band of the Hussars and Light Dragoons but, as we had feared, bands were already being treated as resources to be allocated, with priorities that we would not necessarily agree with. It was, therefore, with much relief that The Band of the Hussars and Light Dragoons was allocated. In addition to being "our band", as importantly, the Band was under the inspirational leadership of David Creswell, well known to most of us, having been the Regiment's last bandmaster. With David Creswell and The Hussars and Light Dragoons Band we had a band that understood the Regiment, embraced the opportunities that the Pipes and Drums brought and was open and ready to consider our suggestions, whilst not being shy in providing sound advice and being ready to push back when ideas were ill advised. Pipe Major Johnston was the partner to David Creswell. His enthusiasm and dedication to the Pipes and Drums had made a vital contribution in establishing the Pipes and Drums central position in the amalgamated Regiment, making it much loved and recognised as being part of the fabric of the new Regiment. As all were to witness the Band and Pipes and Drums were front and centre throughout the weekend and probably the most commented on aspect afterwards. It would be easy to pass too quickly over those who made the Parade itself such a success because it went off without hitch and gave the impression of something that was done with apparent ease. The reality was that the Parade was only the success it was because of the people who made it so and the hard work put in by all involved. The RSM, Tom Hamilton, was the one who planned, rehearsed and made sure it went without fault on the day. I should add that he was masterful in tactfully handling the Commanding Officer's wilder ideas.

Rehearsing in unusually kind North Yorkshire weather. The RSM discusses the finer points of drill with Sgt Garner.

I cannot detail the many key characters on the Parade, all of whom grasped their roles with immense pride, but I must mention Andrew Ledger, the Second in Command and the Squadron Leaders. Andrew, as he has done throughout his career, perhaps with the exception of his very early years when his temper could get the better of him, as his radio equipment was want to find out, was the covert conductor, quietly working behind the scenes to smooth ruffled feathers, to stroke egos and to help find solutions. We did not change to the Northern Ireland ORBAT until after the parade so Cuthy commanded his squadron along with the two, charging young turks, Robert Hutton and Tom Beckett. We all know what happened to Tom and I am sure Robert's career would also have been stellar had he chosen to stay. Providing the ideal balance to these three was Tim Easby, famed for his secretary's line when at the old Western District, that he was "out on business"; which meant that he was off with the South Shropshire on his hunter, Business. Although thoroughly professional, he brought an important lightness to all the preparations. A final mention should go to our Padre, Rory McLeod, who was far from being "our" Padre but he threw himself wholeheartedly into his role and as we shall see, at the Drumhead Service, showed why padres still have an important role to fill. It was, therefore, a splendid team that set out to prepare for and to deliver all parts of the weekend.

Central to the whole occasion were, of course, the Colonel in Chief and Deputy Colonel in Chief. The Colonel in Chief was then 96 and although she continued to appear to be in remarkable health she was clearly frail, and it would not have been surprising if she picked up something that would have prevented her from coming. In the end she was quite amazing and was a commanding presence throughout the day. The twist of fate which had left us in the extremely fortunate position of having Prince Philip as our Deputy Colonel in Chief was a bonus in more ways than one. It not only meant that we were exceptionally blessed in having two senior members of the Royal Family with us, it also meant that if Her Majesty could not attend then we would not be faced with having to postpone the event. The planning needed to take account of what the Colonel in Chief could do. This meant that the inspection would be done using an open top Range Rover and we were told that Her Majesty would not make an address. The Palace and Clarence House were very helpful in making the necessary arrangements and as I recall we really did not need to concern ourselves unduly about the many elements that needed to be put in place, to enable their arrival and departure. Before going on to talk about how things developed it is worth dwelling on the discussions that were had over what form the occasion as a whole would take.

Many of the elements selected themselves but many decisions needed to be made on the optional aspects and of the detail of nearly everything. To start with we needed to decide what we were going to include in the weekend; was it to be just the day or, if not, what else should be included? With all the commanders departing on the Sunday for Folkstone and with a busy spring on the tanks leading up to the date, including firing at Castlemartin and troop training on Salisbury Plain, as well as all the preparation for the Northern Ireland tour, we had to be realistic about what could be included. It was not going to be similar in scale to the Tercentenary celebrations and we needed to be clear on this from the start. Catterick, though, is a long way for most to get to and we quickly recognised that we needed to do something on the Thursday evening and on the Saturday morning. In the end both Messes welcomed the Old Comrades in on the Thursday evening and a barbecue lunch was arranged as the final activity on the Saturday. And what about the day itself; the Parade, lunch and then an evening party surely, but within this lay many possibilities. The format of the Parade largely wrote itself, but I was keen that it should convey who we were and our history and as a result I felt that we must have tanks and horses on the Parade. The RSM very sensibly saw both of these as potential pooh traps; horses did not march in step and tended to react badly to being shouted at and, sadly, as we all know tanks have a habit of breaking down at the most inconvenient of moments. It is rather depressing but the idea that four tanks could be relied upon to move and their gun kits to work was seen as being wildly optimistic. The ideas were discussed and chewed over but the RSM could see I was not going to budge and to my recollection graciously accepted that they would be included. The tanks and Scimitars were easily identified but finding the mounted element proved to be much more challenging. The Household Cavalry did, in the end, come up trumps, providing 2 Blacks, but we had to turn to my wife's show jumper, turned rising dressage horse Crestaleen, to make up the mounted escort. Dinah allowed her to be used with some trepidation, borne as much from concern of how her horse would behave in front of the Queen Mother as she was about anything untoward happening to her. Crestaleen became part of the mounted escort on the strict understanding that she was only to be ridden by Will Griffiths. Dinah had got to know Will's riding well from riding out with the polo ponies in Fallingbostel and was content that, although he played, he did not ride like a polo player. On the drill itself, I was sensible enough to follow well established precedent, until it came to how the Regiment should march off. In order to make the most of the tanks, which by that stage had advanced behind the Regiment and sat in the centre of the square, I suggested that we should march off in a more dramatic way, coming through an arch of the tanks' barrels and then splitting left and right in front of the saluting dais, to march off. This unconventional manoeuvre, needless to say, was not in the drill manual and I think gave the RSM palpitations. Naturally he did not say no but tactfully, in his way, made clear it was not going to happen. In the end we compromised, we did march down the centre, through the elevated barrels of the tanks but then marched across to the edge of the square so that we could march past and off conventionally. When it came to choosing the music I do not remember there being too much to decide. David Creswell knew the Regiment's music so well he would have proposed a programme that could not be bettered. It was a military occasion so inevitably we had a healthy discussion about dress. The options were Number 1 or Number 2 Dress. I think we started from a presumption that it should be Blues, as that would be so much smarter, but when the reality of getting everyone into Blues became apparent it did not take long to accept that the only realistic option was to go for

Number 2 Dress, in all its dullness. I think on the day with the colour and variety that the Royal Party, Band, mounted escort, Pipes and Drums, Guidon Party, Clerics, Orderlies and the armour brought the spectacle was still impressive. The detail of the Parade was, therefore, determined fairly early on although bringing all the elements together continued to present challenges right up until the day. What then of the other parts of the day?

We wanted to ensure that the Regiment and the families felt involved as much as possible. This started after the Parade with a reception for a cross section of those serving in the Regiment and their wives. The Officers' Mess was determined to be the best venue and, as it proved, did provide a relaxed and convivial environment for many from the Regiment and their wives to meet the Colonel and Deputy Colonel in Chief. Lunch needed to be an event for the whole regimental family, those serving, their families and the Old Comrades. The only venue that would enable this was the tank park or as it was called, Megido Lines. The idea to some seemed ridiculous, imbued as they were with memories of only needing to get close enough to see a tank park to come away smelling of oil and diesel and worse. Miraculously Megido Lines had been well built and had been well looked after. The tank park still looked and felt new and Challenger had not deposited the quantities of lubricant onto the floor that its predecessor, Chieftain, would have done. The large bays were big enough to enable one to be used for each Squadron, to sit themselves and all of their guests together, and with doors open and facing each other across the open area it made an ideal venue. With the Colonel in Chief and Deputy Colonel in Chief in the centre it did feel that all were lunching with them. We needed to do a little work to make the bays look their best and this was relatively easily achieved by hanging marquee linings around the walls. The big bonuses were a huge saving on marquees, which would have been the only other option, and the confidence that the solution meant that this part of the programme could handle whatever the Yorkshire weather threw at us on the day. Not involving the evening venues also meant that they could be prepared and made ready in good time. We determined that we needed to do something in the afternoon, to provide another opportunity for more of the Regiment to meet the Deputy Colonel in Chief and to entertain the Old Comrades and families after lunch. Megiddo lines again provided the ideal setting for a range of stands. These gave the squadrons and departments the opportunity to show themselves off and proved to be just what was needed after lunch for the families and Old Comrades. Someone even managed to summon up a Challenger 2 from somewhere. It seems hard to believe now, as we wrestle with upgrades to keep it operationally effective, but back then it was the first time many had seen a Challenger 2.

And so to the evening activities. As I have mentioned we identified that we needed to do something on the first evening, to entertain the Old Comrades. Most of them would have had a long journey and all would be keen to re-establish their bond with the Regiment over a glass of something. The more risk averse thought that whatever we organised would inevitably become a session which would not be the ideal preparation for the following day, but this was thankfully overlooked and both the Officers' and Sergeants' Messes welcomed the Old Comrades. As for the evening following the Parade this would get off to an excellent beginning thanks to the splendid David Creswell who offered to put on a beating retreat. Although this meant that the programme became pretty hectic it did provide the perfect start to the evening. We of course talked about the consequence of rain on both the Parade and Beating Retreat but decided we had to hope for the best and to be prepared to cancel the Beating Retreat if the worst came to the worst. The form of the evening parties again led to much discussion. Should we go for an all ranks bash, a joint officers and sergeants mess event or have separate events. It was numbers and the need to avoid putting up unnecessary marquees, as well as a feeling of what would work best, that led to us decide to go for two main venues. Thanks to its previous training role, Cambrai Barracks offered two ideal locations; Headquarters Squadron organised a party in the Gym and the sabre squadrons one in the NAAFI function rooms. The senior Old Comrades were hosted by the officers in the Officers' Mess and the Sergeants' Mess opened its doors to the Old Comrades later on. Food, if you will pardon the pun, was a vital ingredient to all the events. As I have mentioned we were very fortunate in having a Master Chef full of ideas and ready to consider our ideas, even if unusual. I recall that deciding on the menu for the lunch was a memorable and most enjoyable morning, sampling the suggested menu options. I cannot remember what we tried, only that choosing was not easy and that the summer pudding was particularly good and a clear shoe in. Funnily enough I do not remember vegetarian options being discussed at any stage.

The final piece of the jigsaw was what to do on Saturday. A drumhead service was quickly decided upon, although at the time we did not know Padre Rory well and what he would bring to the occasion. It was decided to round off the whole occasion with a barbecue lunch for all, again back in Megiddo lines.

Having made the key decisions, the organisation and preparation was then taken on by Cuthy's Guidon Team, the QM and RSM whilst the rest of the Regiment concentrated on cramming in those courses that had been postponed thanks to Bosnia and BATUS and that needed to be done before Northern Ireland training commenced. I seem to remember feeling quite relaxed about the state of preparation at that stage. Issues and problems arose but those with the relevant lead always seemed to come up with a solution. The cost was a constant issue and it was only thanks to the solutions that were found, to many of the potentially high cost elements, that we managed to remain within a sensible budget. I cannot remember all the wheezes that were pulled off, but I do recall Paul Hodgson playing a blinder with the Royal Engineers, to have the stands erected, I am sure at no cost to us. As those that sat in them, exposed to the elements on the day, will remember they were, however, not covered. This did cause us some concern as they would be used by many Old Comrades but the alternative would have been an eye watering expense. I remember that visiting Cuth in his office at this time was not always the most reassuring experience. He was only ever positive and eager to explain all that was happening but understanding how the progress that he recited somehow emanated from the apparent total chaos that was his desk was difficult to understand.

I like working in a chaotic way and to have papers strewn around me when immersed in a particular issue, but I usually bring some order to the chaos at the end of the day. For Cuth it seemed a perpetual state of affairs but it worked for him and the proof was in the excellent product he delivered at the end of the day.

Away from the Regiment the essential partner in the preparations was Home Headquarters. Inviting and making all of the necessary arrangements for the Old Comrades was a key piece of the puzzle. We soon recognised that there was a fine balance to be struck in deciding how much the Regiment should take on and how much we needed to leave with individuals. I believe in the end we got it right. Accommodation was potentially a big issue. Should, indeed could, we provide any accommodation and if not, what arrangements did we need to make? Again, I am sure, thanks to the smooth talking of the Quartermaster, some accommodation was found in one of the refurbished transit camps just over the hill. This was spartan but of a good standard and allowed us to at least offer this option. Many Old Comrades found a bed with friends in a married quarter and for the rest we investigated hotel and B & B options and provided the necessary information. Individuals booked the accommodation themselves. Critically this meant that the Guidon Office did not become a travel agency, arranging accommodation. Some I am sure were unhappy that the responsibility for booking their accommodation fell to them, but it was the only practical way to manage that aspect and I believe in the end worked well. Chris Owen and his team did a terrific job in enabling the communication and in obtaining the necessary details from the Old Comrades. This meant that we were as ready as we could be for the onslaught, when they all arrived on the Thursday; supportive, eager to see the Regiment, to experience the camaraderie of the occasion and of course to be looked after appropriately.

The rehearsals for the Parade began in earnest in May. The RSM seemed to come alive at this time. He was never a quiet soul but when we were engaged in the armoured side of our lives he was a supporting presence, a very strong one, but nevertheless he worked largely behind the scenes to keep the show on track.

As soon as rehearsals started his position changed dramatically. The Regiment now largely seemed to be his and thanks to the respect he enjoyed all seemed quite content that this was so. For my part I was largely an observer. I was kept away, ostensibly because I did not need to be involved, but more probably because the RSM wanted to avoid having to deal with any more "helpful" suggestions. This detachment leaves the Commanding Officer in an interesting situation. The Regiment is being drilled within an inch of its life, to reach the peak of perfection, whilst the Commanding Officer is only vaguely aware of what is transpiring from the shouting, stamping of feet and beat of a base drum, heard coming from the drill square. Acutely conscious that he holds centre stage for many parts of the Parade, the Commanding Officer is left to get himself ready. He only joins in at the end of the rehearsals when he needs to able to slot in and be ready to fulfil his role. I had the excellent parade programme which detailed all the movements and the words of command, so the format and my part were clear. All I needed to do was to make sure that I could do all the necessary manoeuvres and remember all the words of command. The only way to achieve this seemed to be the tried and tested process of practice, practice and then more practice. I am sure all those in a similar situation have found the solution that suits them best. For me, I found that, in what was largely a fine spring, the best place to practice was in the quiet and tranquil setting at the back of Haig House, the Commanding Officer's house. The large area of tarmac provided a suitable parade ground and a broom handle or other suitable implement made an adequate sword. Our two sons, Benjamin and Tristan, were at that time just 3 and 2 but still have memories of their father regularly stomping around the back of the house shouting and waving a stick at somebody they could not see. Crestaleen used to lift her head occasionally from her grazing to peer at me with apparent mild amusement whilst our border collie, Triff, initially attempted to bring some order to my antics but soon gave up and returned to her self appointed responsibility of minding Crestaleen. This memory interestingly seems to be the only one which lingers for the boys, 20 years later. It seemed to work and by the time it came for me to take my place on the square I felt confident that I knew my lines and when to give them. I also had to decide how I was going to handle my response to the Colonel in Chief's few words. I could read them off a card which I would need to take out of my pocket or I could try and remember them. It was suggested by one of the young technocrats that I could have an ear piece and be prompted, if necessary, by someone listening from off the square. I am not sure if it proves my Luddite tendencies, but I was not taken by this idea. I could see this going horribly wrong. Simplicity seemed to be the best solution, so I decided to remember the lines and to have a card in my pocket as a back up, in case my memory failed me. I also added a complication by deciding to include a comment about the weather as I felt I had to recall the dreadful weather when Her Majesty had taken the QOH Tercentenary Parade. This meant that I needed to have two options, depending on what the weather did on the day. I anticipated that what the weather would be doing would be apparent early on, enabling me to settle on one of the two options before I went on to the square. In the end the weather was splendidly unpredictable, at one stage looking as if it would be fine and then starting to spit and look more menacing as the start time neared. I, therefore, stepped out unsure of what I was going to say and only later in the parade settled upon the fine weather option. I suspect I have selective memory when it comes to recalling the rehearsals themselves, but I do not remember any major problems arising and, rather, a confidence that it was all looking very good. I seem to remember the RSM not being quite so sanguine and routinely grumbling about someone or something that was not quite right but progress through to the dress rehearsal seemed to pass largely without major incident. Although the drill elements became well practiced the tanks and Scimitars, horses and the Band were not involved in the rehearsals until the final days. Getting the tanks onto the square without destroying it was a challenge that could only be done just before the day. We were though only too well aware that the longer they sat there the less likely it was that they would start. The Blacks only arrived just in time and therefore the mounted escort only joined in rehearsals very late in the day. I do remember that this necessitated the moving of the Band on the first occasion that the Band and horses came together. When they struck up just behind the mounted guard they set Crestaleen cantering off across the square and were duly moved to make them a little less threatening.

And so we arrived at the Dress Rehearsal. My memory tells me that this took place in our neighbour's barracks but on looking back at the photographs it is clearly our barracks. I can only think that we had planned to do it there at some stage. Even though this is a false trail it is a good opportunity to comment on the support that we received from 1 Royal Irish. Their Commanding Officer, Jeremy Brooks was a friend from my days as a platoon commander at Sandhurst and it was a real pleasure to find him in the house next door and his Battalion in the adjoining barracks. Although our programmes hardly crossed we did enjoy an excellent rapport with them and they could not have been more helpful in providing support and assistance for the Parade. The Colonel of the Regiment, Richard Barron, came up in time for the Dress Rehearsal and joined the party that was taking over Haig House. In the end, as well as the four of us, we had my parents, David and Annie Jenkins, Richard and Margret Barron and Tim Lewis tucked away somewhere. It was a busy place, made lively by the presence of two boisterous young boys. Colonel Richard had been keeping in touch throughout the preparations but had not sought to delve into the detail. Once the major elements had been agreed he had largely left me to plan and to put in place the arrangements for the weekend. He was, though, always supportive and I knew that I could seek his opinion if necessary and that I would get helpful advice. By the time we had got to the Dress Rehearsal the die was therefore cast and I did not envisage any change being made. In this I had somewhat misjudged the Colonel. Although relaxed and supportive up to that point, at that rehearsal he was clearly running a critical eye over what was planned and was ready to require change if he felt it was necessary. In the end he identified a few aspects that we needed to address which we duly got on and changed. I am afraid I cannot remember what the issues were. I think I was a little surprised at the time but that was my fault for not anticipating the likelihood that a few things would need to change. The most memorable part of the day of the Dress Rehearsal was though, without doubt, the weather. It poured down only like it can in Yorkshire from start to finish. As we were well aware that we were going to get drenched we did the parade in combats. It was, therefore, an essential if none too pleasant a parade that thankfully did not have a knock effect for the following day. I suspect that, had that been all that was memorable, the event would largely have been forgotten but that was not to be the case. The rehearsal has been stamped into the memory of all who were there because of the stand in for CGS. As we all stood to attention in the pouring rain, licking the drips off the end of our noses, anticipating the arrival of CGS, we were all taken aback when the Pink Panther, or at least someone dressed in a Pink Panther outfit, stepped out of the CGS' limousine. The figure who quickly became as bedraggled as we were played the part with impressive assurance, taking up his position on the saluting dais with appropriate solemnity. It was the erstwhile Charlie Duff who had decided on this moment to unleash the mischievous side of his nature. The reaction unsurprisingly was laughter and lots of it, a much needed tonic on such a dreadful day. I can still recollect struggling to order a General Salute amidst the surrounding mirth. As I recall, the Colonel who must have been equally surprised to find Duff in his outfit waiting for him, also saw the humorous side. With the rehearsals done and the required tweaks made the Regiment took a deep breath and waited for our guests to descend upon us. Ground zero for this was the reception run by the Guidon Office who appeared to masterfully cope with the inevitable unexpected arrivals and changed plans. As far as I could see all eventually departed for their accommodation well briefed and ready for events to unfold.

The two evening events in the Officers' and the Sergeants' Messes did, as was expected, prove to be memorable sessions. Mary and her team were magnificent in coping with such a large number, the night before they had to run lunch the following day for the VVIPs and then a party for 400 in the evening, and the scene in the Sergeants' Mess was apparently even more memorable.

I am told I left at a remarkably sensible hour and it was good to find all capable if not perhaps at their very best the following day. The celebrations had certainly got off to a good start.

And so the day dawned. What was it to bring, the torrential rain of the dress rehearsal or clear skies? It is no wonder that discussing the weather is a Brit's default topic of conversation as it seems to end up dominating so many things that we do. We would of course carry on regardless, but we were all well aware that everyone's enjoyment would be affected by the weather and could curtail what the Colonel in Chief was able to do. The weather in the early part of the day kept us in suspense as to what would unfold later on. Despite the night before I woke fairly early and stepped outside for a final practice before the house woke and I needed to ensure the boys did not wreak too much havoc. In the end they were a great distraction until they departed, to pass into the capable hands of the Kindergarten team. I was well aware that, at that time, a lot was going on but I was content to work on the basis that no news was good news. I then left our senior guests early. They would depart later, to arrive at the appropriate hour but I decided to move into RHQ, to ready myself and just to be there, out of the way, as the key early activity unfolded. I remember wondering how the Royal Party was getting on but of course their arrangements are so well oiled this was going to be the last element that was going to go wrong. It was at this stage that I had expected to be able to settle on which of the variations I was going to use in my address, but the weather was holding us in suspense. One minute it looked as if it was going to clear and then the skies darkened and there was rain in the air. I also found myself vacillating over when to go out and to get into position. I did not want to be rushed but I also did not want to be standing around for too long. In the end I judged it about right and walked round to the top of the square with a light rain falling. Despite this the inherently optimistic temperament, which I still had at that time, caused me to conclude that the skies did not look too threatening. I seem to remember having time to meet a few of the more senior guests and to take in the stands which all looked to be pretty packed. The Kindergarten was in position at the front, but I do not remember spotting either of the boys. I was reminded at this point that it was not just those of us on parade that were under scrutiny; one senior officer being informed by an even more senior officer that he should not be wearing a recently awarded neck decoration and my successor in command, still getting used to a tent hat, being caught with his on back to front. Then came the first barked command and the Regiment marched on. We were off, and the rain seemed to have stopped. I stepped out on to the square and marched out to take over command from Andrew Ledger who, as is the protocol, informed me how many officers and men were on parade. I of course took no notice of the numbers but was pleased that he did not add "and 2 Smith boys" as he had when handing over to me on Paddy's Day. The two youngest members of the family had thankfully remained with the Kindergarten on this occasion.

As with any well rehearsed event, from a participants point of view, the Parade unfolded as was anticipated. I was thankful that it did so and that there were no major surprises. My solitary rehearsals in the garden proved their worth and as far as I can recall I managed to deliver the correct commands and to do everything at the right time, without any moments of consternation. Everyone involved played their part and delivered their lines exactly as required, delivering a fine spectacle to those watching on. I am, therefore, unaware of any glitches or anecdotes, amusing or otherwise, that I can reveal. Tom may well have some but none that he chose to share after the event. I do, though, retain many fond memories of a day made very special by the presence and contribution of two towering characters in the recent life of the Nation. We were incredibly fortunate that both the Queen Mother and Prince Philip graced us with their presence and that the Queen Mother was able to participate so fully. Unsurprisingly with Her Majesty being in her 97th year we had been warned that her participation would be limited. On the day she belied her years and took a full part; climbing up into and then standing in the cut down Range Rover to review the Regiment, walking out to play a full part in the blessing of the new Guidon and delivering a personal address that she had so clearly composed herself. I suspect most find it difficult to adequately express the impact of such a contribution, but I have no doubt that all of us felt fortunate to be on the Parade and that those watching felt very privileged to have been there that day. The unpredictability of what exactly was going to happen added a not unwelcome touch of spice and left some memorable images. The Equerry going out with both sword and furled brolly was one; ready to protect against all eventualities.

As for other memories, there are a few that linger and that are probably best recalled as they unfolded. The arrival of the Royal Party with the mounted escort looked as splendid as we had hoped. Crestaleen was clearly a handful for Will which he handled with great aplomb, by seemingly allowing her to turn to take in all that was going on around her, her athletic exuberance contrasting splendidly with the solid, unruffled steadiness of the two Blacks. She made her mark on the Queen Mother who much to Dinah's delight commented afterwards what a beautiful horse she was.

With all settled and the review completed it was C Squadron's turn to take centre stage. Whether it was Tom Becket's competitive edge or Mick Broom's expertise at drill, I suspect the former, C Squadron won the drill competition and as a result the privilege of trooping the old Guidons. They did not disappoint and were impressively sharp. The eventual departure of the old Guidons was a surprisingly moving moment. Even though oft rehearsed their final departure to Auld Lang Syne was very poignant for all those from The Queen's Own Hussars and from The Queen's Royal Irish Hussars who were on parade and I am sure felt equally and possibly more strongly by those sitting in the stands, marking as it did that moment when the two Regiments formally became part of the history of The Queen's Royal Hussars.

It was at about this stage that there was an unscripted clatter as one of the 2 orderlies, in full ceremonial dress and positioned either side of the saluting dais, feinted. I know having chatted to him afterwards that he was mortified and I have huge sympathy for him. The two were selected for their size, as there are few who can still fit into the ceremonial uniforms that we have, and it was good of them to take on the role. The uniform was not best suited to having to stand throughout the Parade, with nothing to break the monotony of their solitary vigil, but they added an important element to the overall tapestry. Such occurrences are part and parcel of parades and just add to the depth of the memory. I trust he now remembers it with good humour and has managed to dine out on the story or at least to prop up a bar with it a few times.

The forming of a hollow square, or at least an open sided hollow square, was very effective, as was intended, in creating an intimate setting for the consecration of the new Guidon and the ceremony itself provided the appropriate gravitas for such a significant moment. It was also splendid that it provided the opportunity for the Second in Command and Quartermaster to be centre stage, as they uncased the Guidon and placed it on the drums. Andrew Ledger indeed featured on the photograph of the day which was of course the Colonel in Chief dedicating the new Guidon. It was during the Service that I finally felt confident that the day was going to stay fine and that I could remark in my address on how joyous we were that, unlike when Her Majesty was last on the square, that the sun had chosen to shine on her that day. After the soaking of the previous day I am sure I sensed, if I did not hear, a murmuring of agreement from the massed ranks around me.

The reforming and then the march past all went off well, with the left forms rather than wheeling around the corners adding greatly to the spectacle and being testament to both the RSM's ambition and ability to get the Regiment to do it to such a consistently high standard. As we came back into line I was tuned in to the tanks, whose cue it was to start up their engines. As I stood watching the Regiment complete the manoeuvre I was able to count a reassuring cloud of smoke, although thankfully not Chieftain like in nature, rising from each of the four tanks. At that stage I had my fingers crossed that all the gun kits also fired up. It is difficult to imagine now after 15 years of Challenger 2 technology that Challenger 1's turret was still basically a Chieftain turret with Chobham armour and, therefore, although not quite steam driven, was still valve technology. They did all start up without trouble and it was splendid to hear the roar of the engines and clank of track as the tanks and Scimitars advanced behind the Regiment, to complete the advance in review order. At that point I felt that the risk had paid off. The impact that they had when they advanced, when they dipped their barrels as part of the Royal Salute and in forming an arch with their barrels for the Regiment to march through and off the square, all provided an unusual if not unique dimension to the Parade, that spoke to what the Regiment was. I hope that the impression that was left was that we can do the ceremonial well but do not forget what we are, an armoured regiment.

And so it was all over. It had gone well and all, I think, stood tall afterwards, proud to have been involved; for the most part accepting that all the preparation and rehearsal had been worthwhile. There was, however, no time to dwell on what had happened as rifles and swords needed to be locked away and for all to become hosts for the Reception and Lunch. Although the Royal Party took a few minutes out our other senior guests were soon arriving in the Officers' Mess. I recall greeting CGS, Roger Wheeler, who it was good to see, seemed to be in excellent spirits. Although not planned he was nevertheless hugely impressed that Killaloe had been one of the tunes that had been played as we marched past. I am sure I just accepted the praise as if it had all been intended. The reception itself went very well and succeeded in enabling a good cross section of the Regiment and their wives to meet The Queen Mother and Prince Philip. We had arranged it so that we had two lots of groups, gathered separately, with The Queen Mother meeting those in the dining room and Prince Philip those in the ante room. We had estimated that there should be just enough time for all of the groups to be introduced and The Queen Mother allowed me to escort her around the groups in the dining room at a pace that achieved that. There was, however, consternation about half way through the allocated time when it became apparent that Prince Philip had whistled around his groups and had marched across to the dining room to see what was happening there. Of course, it mattered not and it just meant that many in the dining room were fortunate enough to have the opportunity to be introduced to both The Queen Mother and Prince Philip but it seemed to throw some. The action then moved up to Megido lines for lunch. With the weather fine, the doors open and the bays suitably decorated the tank park proved to be a splendid venue. The wine flowed, the banter sparked and I think everyone felt part of the same occasion. I was kept on my toes at lunch, being sent off by The Queen Mother to change places with the Lord Mayor of Birmingham at one point so that she could be the focus of attention for a little while. As far as I can remember the menu, selected with such care, although hardly touched by Her Majesty seemed to go down well. After the lunch The Queen Mother again surprised us by strolling around the Squadrons to meet many of the Old Comrades and guests, leaving many more with a cherished memory of a brief moment in her beguiling company. Prince Philip as energetic as ever was very happy to be taken around the stands that the Squadrons had put together, to give the guests an insight into the life of the Regiment. His genuine interest was greatly appreciated and all those on the stands revelled in being able to explain what they were showing off, none more so than the Pipes and Drums. I had the devil of a job in prizing Prince Philip away from Cpl Massey, LCpl Foley and Tpr Findlay. Eventually I managed to extract Prince Philip so that we could meet up again with The Colonel in Chief for the photographs. Wet weather alternatives had been planned for in the hangers but thankfully we were able to have both the Officers' and Sergeants' Mess photographs taken in the sunshine. And so we reached the end of the Royal Visit, with the final act being the presentation of posies by three daughters of serving members of the Regiment.

The party though had only just started, with a full evening to follow. I certainly felt like celebrating and it did seem that what unfolded enabled all, both guests and hosts, to relax and enjoy themselves. A tactical pause allowed everyone to return to wherever they were staying, to change and ready themselves for the evening. Suitably reshod all returned to the square and the stands for the Beating Retreat. Thankfully the weather continued to improve and we were able to enjoy, in the evening sun, a really outstanding example of what can be achieved when flair and excellence complement each other so effectively. David Creswell brought together brilliantly the full range of his own Band with that of the Pipes and Drums, to deliver a display that was so very much greater than the sum of the two quite excellent parts. We were not to be left feeling disappointed at an opportunity missed but full of admiration for an outstanding display of what can be achieved when Band and Pipes complement each other. The Pipes and Drums were able to play their full part as they had on the Parade. Thanks to Tom Becket's stewardship and Pipe Major Johnston's drive the Pipes and Drums had gone from strength to strength, numbering nine pipers and 5 drummers at the time of the Parade. I will not try and review the programme of music which saw the audience sitting in rapt attention, tapping their feet and joining in vigorously during Killaloe except to comment on my two particular favourites. The haunting melodies, Emerald Echoes and Carlingford Loch, written by David Creswell, so unique to the Regiment and played so evocatively that evening are a lasting memory of not only that evening but also of that privileged time when the Regiment had both Band and Pipes and, which, when in the hands of someone with David Creswell's talent were able to produce such magnificent music.

I cannot move on without also mentioning the impromptu drive by of the portaloos. Within the complex administrative web of the whole event some portaloos had needed to be moved from Megiddo lines that evening and it just happened that this occurred, quite by accident, right in the middle of the Beating Retreat. Not surprisingly their passage across the bottom of the square was the cause of much laughter and pointing. Had the Band been aware of what was happening they would have laughed along with the spectators but as the portaloos passed behind and unknown to them the spectators' reaction must have been somewhat disconcerting. They had clearly encountered worse and were not put off their stride one jot and if any offence was taken it was quickly dispelled afterwards when what had occurred was explained. The intervention added to, rather than detracted from, the memories of the event, which, when I reflect on them, give me cause to feel privileged to have been able to experience such a memorable occasion.

The evening having been got off to the best of starts all then dispersed to the three venues for the parties. The party in the

Officers' Mess was very lively. The Officers, not that they needed an excuse, were glad to be celebrating a successful day and the Old Comrades were keen to carry on the motion. In the vain hope that all of the 400 present would be able to enjoy warm food that they could look forward to eating rather than to eat to just satisfy their hunger I had suggested that we have an individual chateaubriand for each table. The cooking and serving was done perfectly by the chefs and Mary's team, the challenge came in the carving. Many managed with great aplomb but there were one or two tables which seemed to find the challenge a little testing. Overall it seemed to go down well and certainly added to the fun. I did venture across to the other parties and was pleased to find them in full swing late into the evening. I was nearly snared but managed to withdraw in reasonably good order. I also remember one or two rather underdressed characters coming the other way and making an appearance in the Officers' Mess. I think they took one look and then headed back. The evening rolled on and naturally petered out as fatigue, age, the protestations of wives or the effect of what had been imbibed took its toll. I usually find myself enjoying that phase, when the fire has died down but the embers are still glowing and, as I was in the fortunate position of being able to see Dinah off home in the staff car, that particular tug was missing so I could remain. As a consequence, I believe I was one the last few standing, I am sure much to the annoyance of the young, but such occasions do not come around too often and need to be savoured to the last.

Following well established tradition we were all up at a reasonable hour the next day, to get ready for the Drumhead Service. For some it must have felt like penance but most looked to be in surprisingly good shape as they formed up. The weather, sadly, had reverted to type and meant that we needed to retreat indoors. I remember a call from the RSM and agreeing that we would have to go for the wet weather option. Thankfully the splendid new technical accommodation again came to the rescue. The individual tank bays were not large enough to accommodate the Regiment and all our guests so we turned to the Workshop whose cavernous building made an ideal venue once the necessary seating had been put in for the Old Comrades and families. Despite the austere setting the Service was moving and memorable, even for many who would normally be left uninspired by such occasions, thanks again to another notable contribution. Shrinking numbers had long since consigned to history the concept of the regimental padre and it was not easy for any padre to make a strong connection with a regiment for one off events. We were, though, very fortunate to find ourselves with Rory McLeod looking after us. Charming, supportive and ready to assist in whatever way he could Rory had been a great help in the preparation for the whole event but, until the Drumhead Service, I had failed to appreciate what Rory would bring to the occasion and was, like many, unprepared for his masterful handling of the Service and his deeply moving address, which went way beyond normal expectation. I have often wished that I could recall his words. Sadly, I can only remember being moved myself and being full of admiration for how Rory, seemingly, managed to carry the whole congregation with him as he wove his address. The Service will be recalled by many as a significant part of the whole three days, providing as it did a fitting conclusion to the formal events.

All that was left was to wander down to the barbecue, which provided a suitably relaxed and informal opportunity, to share a little food and drink before the Old Comrades and our other guests departed. I do not recollect the weather dampening proceedings, so the rain must have passed by. Oh, the joys of being based in Yorkshire. The raffle for which NATO cars had kindly presented a Rover 100 as the prize was drawn and most thought it very just when Tpr Ramsey was drawn as the lucky winner, having only recently written his car off.

The events thus drew to a close and all that was left was to say farewell to our guests. There was no time to dwell on what had happened as eyes quickly turned to focus on preparation for the Northern Ireland tour and most immediately to driving down to Folkstone for the Commanders' Cadre, followed by the Main Recce to the Province.

Writing this account of the preparations and of the events themselves has been a happy journey back down memory lane.

Although often touched upon at various times over the years, reminiscences have only been brief and it has been fascinating to remind myself of what happened and more importantly who was involved. I hope that my recollection of events is accurate and that I have not upset anyone by getting it wrong or, in particular, failing to mention someone that I should have done. If I have, I have no doubt that I will find out quickly enough. Although I did appreciate it at the time, subsequent experience has made me realise more clearly quite how fortunate I was with the team that I had around me then. In that period after amalgamation the Regiment was unusually rich in the quality of those that held nearly all of the key appointments and I have been reminded very strongly of that. I hope that all those who contributed so much to the success of the occasion look back with satisfaction at what they achieved. They all have good cause to do so. As for all of us that were present at Regimental Duty at the time I believe we were all very fortunate that the presentation of the Guidon happened on our watch. Some would have had cause to ponder whether that was the case when it became known when it would be but I doubt there was anyone who, after the event, did not feel fortunate to have been there. I feel very privileged to have been in command at the time. Although not suggesting any comparison I find myself drawing on the sentiment expressed by Seb Coe when he signed off at the end of the 2012 Olympics. I feel all involved should feel a sense of pride in what was achieved and that we did it well.

Post Script – RSM

The last time I had taken part in anything similar was the QOH tercentenary parade, so this parade followed much the same format for the simple reason that I had a video of the tercentenary parade. A few things had changed in the intervening years. Recruits were no longer taught marching in slow time or taught "forming" at all. As the parade was to include forming and slow time we had our work cut out. Early in the preparatory period I received a phone call from London District offering to loan me some drill instructors. I replied "no" as I was positive that QRH could deliver a parade every bit as good as anyone else without having to say it was because "the Guards had helped us out." Early in the year we held a drill competition which did a lot to get everyone into slow time and formings. When it came to the time to bring the Regiment together it was obvious there was still a lot to do. I used one of the members of the Pipes and Drums to bash the base drum and (slowly) we learned to march in time to a drum beat. Drill has never been a Cavalry area of expertise and when the Regiment was lined up you could see twitching and scratching and movement from every Squadron. I spoke to one of the boys and told him, "Blakey. I am going to march over to you, bollock you for moving, then tell you to remove your hat, then I'm going to thump you. OK?" Blakey, none too convinced, agreed. The Regiment marched on. I shouted there was too much movement, picked on Blakey and thumped him (very gently) on top of the head. Blakey should have got an Oscar for his acting. The majority of the Regiment took a deep breath and movement in the ranks disappeared.

The Officers were also required to do sword drill. Most had not touched a sword since their one lesson at Sandhurst, so I had to teach them. I had not touched a sword at all! I took my RSMs sword home together with a drill manual and practised endlessly in my front room. One particular drill movement (Salute in slow time) sees you thrust the sword away from you "outwards and upwards". This is great and very smart. Practising in a front room with a low ceiling is neither great nor smart. Having thrust my sword "outwards and upwards" it jammed neatly into the plaster of my ceiling, pulling a large chunk of it out when I tried to remove it!

The Guidon of The Queen's Royal Hussars on parade.

DISCIPLINE SINGAPORE STYLE – 1963

William Stewart Singapore, Neesoon camp, me as escort to Tpr Francis Laverty, on orders for being absent from 1st parade. Sqn Ldr. John Paley. "Why were you absent from 1st parade Laverty?"

Laverty "Sir I was with one of the virgins from virgin's corner last night and over slept"

Sqn Leader (head in his hands then shakes his head), "Laverty, they wheeled out the last virgin from virgins corner in a barrow before the Japs invaded in 42. I award you 14 days march out."

Bill Stewart Troop Cpl QRIH Singapore

Same Frances Laverty, months later in Semengo Camp, Malaysia. On Orders for being drunk on parade. Squadron Leader Randall Cooke asked Laverty would he accept his award, Laverty agreed. Sqn leader said 28 days stoppage of 'beer' instead of 'Pay'. Laverty fainted. SSM David (Taffy) Jones ordered 'Carry Out' (very apt)' instead of March Out. The whole camp was in uproar at seeing the escort carrying poor Frances out.

George Moors Troop L/Cpl QRIH Semengo Camp

BOSNIA 1995-96

The Regiment was firing on Castlemartin ranges when news first came out that it was to deploy to Bosnia. There had been a UN force in Bosnia for several years trying to keep the Serbs, Croats and Bosnian muslims apart but it had been a toothless force. For some time, talks had been taking place about the "Dayton" agreement but none of us really knew what that would mean nor what the composition of any NATO force would be. Then, there it was. Get your kit sorted, six weeks, your off. Part of IFOR, the NATO Implementation Force.

Training started straight away. Tanks needed to be prepared and quickly. All the normal checks had to be done and done again. Broken tanks got their spares. Clothing issues took place. Goretex waterproofs, Goretex lined boots known as the Pro boot, Fleeces in DPM (Disruptive Pattern Material), Goretex mits, arctic gloves, white face masks and woolly hats that folded down at the sides so the ears were protected.

The tanks loaded at Teeside docks onto a huge Russian (!) vessel named the Yuri Maksarov or something close to it. A guard party travelled on the ship with orders that no one who was not entitled got into a tank. Moving the tanks around the dock was not fun. There had been heavy snow and the ground was icy.

All too soon the advance party was off. They went over just before Christmas. One of them rang me in the Warrant Officers and Sergeants mess from Kupres during the New Years party and all I could hear in the background was gunfire. This I was assured (but not reassured) to hear was celebratory gunfire. We found out that we would be under the Command of a Canadian Brigade in the North West of Bosnia, not far from Bihac. It was an area that had seen some of the heaviest fighting throughout the war. The Dayton agreement had instructed the warring factions to pull back to either side of a 10 kilometre wide zone of separation (ZOS). The Bosnian (mainly Muslim forces) would be to the south of the zone in our area and the Bosnian Serb forces would be to the north of it. The Croat forces were to stay within the borders of Croatia. Our role would be to ensure that all sides stuck to the agreement. The Battle Group was an eclectic mix and consisted of QRH personnel, a Canadian Infantry Company, some combat engineers, a Dutch mortar platoon, a couple of Australians, a New Zealander and a US "Psychological ops" team whose role it would appear was to drive round in a Humvee that was equipped with very large loud speakers. A troop from B Squadron was deployed to Sanski Most in support of a Company of Light Infantry.

In early January we deployed and flew into Split in Croatia. We were then moved into transit accommodation (called the Dalma Warehouse) for the night. It was a large warehouse that had been split into sections by temporary walls about eight feet high. As the warehouse was about thirty feet high the walls gave a semblance of privacy but did nothing to cover noise. Resting there were all those from our flight, some Royal Military Police, a few other personnel from deploying units and a number of the Royal Logistics Corps personnel who worked from the area of the Dalma warehouse sending supplies up country.

I have rarely been unimpressed by members of the British Army. Sadly, I was hugely unimpressed with the members of the Royal Logistic Corps (RLC) in the location at that time. Those we saw that first night were a mass of drunks. They were taking great pleasure in making as much noise as they could and winding everybody up, particularly the RMP (usually good sport but not when a Battle Group is in town waiting to go up country). I tried my best to ignore the noise and had my portable CD player headphones in (it was a long time ago!) listening to music but when some of our Battle Group asked me to intervene it was clear that the drunks were going too far. The rabble seemed to be being led by a large female. When asked to desist she did not. I asked again and was ignored. It is surprising how quickly a Blackthorn can change attitudes when the threat of it being forced up a nostril is introduced. It certainly achieved a comical cross-eyed look from the girl (the Blackthorn is the stick carried by all QRH Warrant Officers). I growled at a couple of other "loggys" who backed off. The rabble and the female disappeared. Peace was restored. It had long been rumoured that members of the RLC were flown into theatre for just over the minimum qualifying period for a medal. From what some of them said that night this was the case with those that had been causing the nuisance. The next morning their RSM asked for a few words and tried to ask why I had growled at his personnel and not come to him. Good on him for sticking up for his troops. I gave him short shrift. My "I'm unimpressed with the RLC" head came off later during the tour. They drove in atrocious conditions for long periods and at considerable risk. Once the supply chain was set up they worked hard to ensure we were looked after. It is a shame that on occasion a few youngsters can let down a Corps by being stupid. Been there, seen it, got the T shirt!

From Dalma we moved up country to Kupres. The town emerged from a thick mist. It was a scene of total devastation. The shattered shells of houses were seemingly all that remained but somehow there was a factory building that was still in reasonable condition. This building was our home overnight. The troops bedded down in a large hall which was freezing cold, but we were fed and there were some toilets installed by the engineers. I found myself a small cupboard and arranged a bed by balancing a large plank (wooden one, not a gunner!) between two shelfs.

The next day the tanks arrived and were "bombed up". It was not a full bomb load, a few live HESH and a few thousand rounds of machine gun ammunition. I was able to stand on a high wall and watch the process take place just below me. The QM, Captain Paul Hodgson, had certainly orchestrated a ballet and the whole thing seemed to pass off without incident.

A recce party consisting of the 2IC, myself and others pushed further up country, eventually arriving at a destroyed village called Krnjeusa. We looked it over to see if it was suitable for the head-quarters and a squadron. It was as we were discussing whether or not we could provide a defensive perimeter that I took a pace backwards and stepped in a dog. It was very dead and under snow and as I stepped back it burst. Bad smell. Not good. The recce decided against Krnjeusa and we decided on a factory complex outside the town of Bosanski Petrovac. This was about as far up the supply chain as it was possible to go and well out in the sticks.

"Bos P" as it came to be called was one long hanger split into a number of repair garages. It also had a small out building with a couple of rooms which became the OCs residence. There was room for some accommodation, but it was limited to those organisations that needed to utilise the buildings such as A Squadron SQMS, LAD and the chefs. Everyone else would be in tents. Once the decision was made to move in, the majority of A Squadron, HQ Squadron and RHQ moved up. Initially there were rows of 9x9 tents and some larger 12x12 tents, as well as personnel sleeping in the hanger (supposedly a bus factory before the conflict). There were no toilets and no washing facilities. Control was needed. It came in the form of Frank. There were two notable Franks in Bos P. Frank the Dutch mortar platoon commander and Frank Davies, HQ Squadron SSM and it is this Frank I write about. Frank arranged the digging of temporary toilets and policed the camp. Frank was a star. Diligent and very funny, although very often he did not realise he was being funny. During parade on one of the early days in Bos P he announced that he was unimpressed with the number of yellow stains in the snow there were outside tents and that if he caught anyone "leaking" outside a tent he would sort them. For the next few nights I diligently got dressed in my cold weather gear (it was very below zero at night) and made my way to the latrines. One night however, having got dressed I stepped outside the 9x9 I was sharing with the Int Warrant Officer and noted a dark figure emerging from his tent. He moved a few feet nearer another tent and then "leaked". For the next few weeks everyone kept a look out to prevent anyone "leaking" near their tent whilst trying their best not to be caught leaking on someone else's!

As Bos P was at such a distance from Split and as the RLC vehicles had to visit a number of locations before getting to us it became evident that food (among other items of stores) was being misdirected from the supply vehicles as they came up country. This was a serious problem. It is rumoured that the Master Chef (WO2 John Jenkinson) borrowed some 4 tonners and headed for Split. Once near Split it is rumoured that he turned his WO2 rank slide round to reveal a Lieutenant Colonels rank slide and then ordered a large quantity of food to be loaded onto the trucks. Of course, I would never believe such a rumour but somehow or another after a few days the quantity and quality of food improved considerably and was excellent for the rest of the tour. The chefs in Bosnia really did the business and managed to deal with any crisis or jump in numbers.

Whilst A Squadron and the support elements of the Battlegroup settled into Bos P, B Squadron was moving into another old factory complex (the shoe factory) in Mrkonjic Grad. One of their troops was deployed to Sanski Most in support of a Light Infantry Company. The mine complex and buildings they occupied had, until just before the implementation of the Dayton agreement been the site of a Serb concentration camp and had been on television showing how badly Bosnian muslims were being treated.

The 2IC continued to look for a suitable, central site for the Battle Group Headquarters and eventually settled on a factory complex in the town of Kljuc. It had a number of advantages. It was well away from the Canadian Brigade Headquarters but not too far from 4 Brigade Headquarters (then under the Command of Brigadier Dannett) so we could have a British umbrella. It was about mid-way between Bos P and Mrkonjic Grad and the Canadian Infantry Company attached to the Battlegroup was already in the town. Getting the selected site ready for occupation was a dirty job. The warring factions did not appear to use toilets. They used old factory buildings! Many of the buildings were full of what people leave behind, rotting vegetables and tons of old paperwork. Windows were missing. In common with Bos P there were no toilet facilities and there were dead animals all over the place. Mostly these were pigs but there was also a cow. It all had to be moved and burned or buried. As quite a bit of Bosnia at this time was a minefield and wandering around outside the perimeter was not a good plan, burning seemed the most obvious action. A huge fire was lit in the middle of the complex and a team worked tirelessly to get the place ready. The fire burned for four days and nights. A couple of days into the clean up I heard a shout of "RSM!" Looking around I saw the Signals and Int Warrant

Officers standing over the dead cow. For some reason that was not immediately apparent they were in possession of a chain saw. It is of note that by now (late January) it was very cold indeed and much of the landscape was frozen and anything like dead flesh was deep frozen. It became clear what the chainsaw was for as it was lowered toward the dead cow and then bit into it. Dead flesh was deep frozen, but not complete cows. The outer couple of inches were frozen. When intestines began flying about it became clear how not frozen the cow was. Somehow it was cut up and somehow it was dragged to the fire.

Another benefit of the factory location in Kljuc was that it had two real toilets, porcelain toilets. It is amazing how desperately you can seek comfort and in what things you can find it. Porcelain toilets were definitely a very high priority comfort. Getting them working was a story in itself which is in other publications but get them working we did. The CO and RHQ moved into Kljuc and there followed a significant number of visits. Whilst the visits went on, the Padre (David Peachell) continued his task of looking after our spiritual guidance and built a bar which became known as Chippies bar and one of the more popular locations in the North West of Bosnia.

In Bos P and several other locations, a new string of inventions was appearing. As there were no showers or proper wash facilities the troops came up with ideas of their own. One (Sgt Leonards invention) was located in one of the maintenance pits and comprised a round tank above head level that was perforated and when hot water was ready it was tipped into the round tank. It worked. Another appeared on national news where SSgt Sparks had come up with a sort of warm jacuzzi at one of the ZOS monitoring sites called Bondi Beach.

Another invention in Bos P comprised a metal bath, under which a fire was lit. Before taking a shower, you added cold water to the tub and then stood in it. The water heated up and then, using a small hand operated pump, was forced up a pipe and out of a shower head. As the water became hotter you added more water into the bath thus keeping the system going and the temperature bearable. Easy one would think. Not for one particular infantry man. He came running out of his tent wrapped in his towel (temperature somewhere about minus 8 to minus 12), jumped into the bath and started pumping. Water went up the pipe and out of the shower head. He made lots of, "Oooh! Ooooh! Ohhh! Bloody 'ell!" noises and got progressively pinker. He finished quickly, shouted "fuck me that was hot!" and ran to his tent. Hot! The water in the bath was actually bubbling! He had added no cold water at any stage. That lad was hard!

At Sanski Most the day of the tanks arrival came. The local Bosnian militia had heard they were coming and were standing outside a building next to the road. These boys had seen it all in the previous years. The first vehicle to arrive was a Spartan (part of the CVRT family). There was some derision at this but then grudging admiration as a Warrior came around the corner. When the ground began to shake the Bosnians did not understand why until a Challenger came into view at speed. They may have thought they had seen everything, but this monster was a whole new ball game. Jaws just dropped. I walked back to my vehicle with a good degree of satisfaction. It disappeared as I got into the factory complex. Conditions were not good. The place smelled like a urinal (the cellars were being used as toilets by the soldiers occupying the buildings) and the infantry that were occupying the place had removed any timber they could find to stoke fires. This included any wooden flooring, so they were sleeping on concrete and having burned the window frames they had nothing to nail heavy duty plastic covering to to provide shelter from the wind. The QRH soldiers had moved into a building a little way from the rest and were making the best of it. I left Sanski Most surprised that not more had been done to make the place comfortable. Brigadier Dannet was equally unimpressed because very shortly after I had returned to Kljuc he arrived and as I was talking to the CO he instructed me to "Go and sack that Company Sergeant Major". I would happily have done so but the CO was more aware of the politics and dealt with the matter via the CO of the unit concerned.

Snow continued to fall and temperatures continued to drop. In order to ensure the Challengers could grip the roads every fourth track pad was removed. It worked. No Challengers fell off any of the precipitous cliffs along which some roads ran (although one did try and was held up by only a sapling!). One troop leader took his tanks on patrol and for reasons beyond my understanding did nearly 100 kilometres. As far as I am aware the majority of military genius' had said tanks could not operate in this terrain. They did, and very well.

On a patrol close to the ZOS a tank crew came across a Bosnian Serb guard manning a small wooden barrier. He stopped the tank and was refusing to let it pass. He drew his pistol. The turret traversed and the main armament muzzle ended up about a foot from his nose. Discretion became the better part of valour and the tank moved on as the Serb returned to his own lines.

Several days after occupying Kljuc a comic type publication began to circulate. It had not been vetted. There was some mickey taking out of the RHQ personalities which in a couple of cases raised some eyebrows. The first copy of "Walter" had been published. Ken Davidson, John Heavey and other members of RHQ troop had devised, printed and circulated this publication which was the Battle Group equivalent of Punch. They produced numerous editions, all uncensored and they derided everyone and everything. It was very clever, could easily have been professional and kept everyone's feet on the ground.

In Mrkonjic Grad one of the troop leaders (I think Lieutenant Sunderland) thought that his soldiers were lonely and therefore decided that welfare support was needed. He wrote to the News of the World newspaper who put out a request for penfriends. Within days the entire military postal service in Bosnia was overwhelmed. Sacks full of mail arrived on a daily basis, thousands of letters. They were shared out around the B Squadron members, the RRF personnel on site and many letters made their way to Kljuc and Bos P. Young women were making some very strange offers and sending very revealing photographs. Eventually it all settled down, but B Squadron continued to get more mail than any other unit for much of the tour and at least one wedding took place as a result of these letters.

Several days after occupying the site in Kljuc a strange banging could be heard from some of the factory buildings behind the

RHQ location. On investigation there was amazement when four elderly people were found to be repairing a world war two era T34 tank. The engine was out, hanging by chains and they had been welding something to do with the brakes in the back decks of the vehicle. As there should have been no former warring factions or their equipment within the zone of separation this was definitely a "no no". On being told that they would lose the tank unless they went, they smiled and took bolt cutters to the chain holding the engine which promptly dropped neatly into place. A couple of minutes with a spanner and one of them jumped in and started her up. After a quick photo shoot with a Challenger, off they went.

By the end of February the Battlegroup was getting to grips with the surrounding area. We knew what to do and what not to do in terms of where to go and what to touch. Bodies were being found almost everywhere, many of them showing signs of violent death. We were supposed to report the location of the bodies so that the war crimes organisation could investigate. Whilst standing close to the entrance gate at Bos P one day I heard a rapid knocking noise, a kind of slap, slap, slap, slap. Turning I saw a Spartan drive past. On top of the Spartan was a plank and on the plank was a deep frozen body. As the Spartan went over the regularly rutted ground the body and the plank would part company and then collide, thus the slapping noise. As almost all of us were by now used to the sight of bodies. It was, in a ghoulish way, very funny.

As well as unfortunate individuals lying in the fields there were several mass graves in the area where, for the most part Bosnian Muslims had been executed by other warring factions. One of these was on the way to an outstation called Bondi Beach. Mud had been bulldozed over a number of bodies. Now, a long time after the event, erosion and the weather were playing their part and bits of body were beginning to stick out of the ground. These had been covered by black plastic bags. As I passed one day I noted a bag flapping in the wind. I went over to secure it and saw a tiny foot in a blue and yellow sock. I would judge the age of the child that was buried there at no more than three. It still gives me occasional nightmares.

On March 17th the Regiment celebrated Paddies Day. Somehow, we had managed to get Shamrock from the UK to Bosnia and kept it in reasonably presentable condition. Martin Bell, a noted journalist who had worked with The Queens Royal Irish Hussars during the Gulf War visited and we toured the locations giving out "Gunfire" or at least copious amounts of Bushmills Whiskey.

By mid tour the snow was melting. One individual was making his way from Kljuc to Sanski Most to visit the Reconnaissance troop soldiers there. On the way he spotted a donkey with a rope around its neck sticking its head out of a burned out building. Jumping out of the Land Rover he was in he managed to get the rope off the donkey. On his way back to the vehicle he felt something odd under his foot. Looking down he could see the edge of a plastic mine called a TMRP 6 sticking out from the underside of his boot. The TMRP 6 is an anti-tank mine and took a fair bit of pressure to set it off. Having told his driver he thought he was on a mine he then said, "It's a TMRP 6. I'm going to step off it." He looked down and breathed deeply and then, hearing a noise, looked up. The Land Rover and its driver were reversing rapidly! The mine did not go bang. The individual and the driver kept quiet. Not everyone escaped the mines. One of our vehicles ran over an anti personnel mine washed into a track by heavy rain. Thankfully no one was hurt but tragically the brother of one of our officers, and his crew with The Light Dragoons were killed just south of our area.

As the weather improved more foot patrols took place. Local Bosnians were returning to rebuild. Every house had to be rebuilt. The retreating warring factions had burned almost every house in the country side. Urban areas had fared a little better. Foot patrols gave some reassurance. More bodies were found and reported. In Mrkonjic Grad Bosnians, intent on proving to the world that Serbs had committed atrocities had dug up almost everyone in a cemetery only 100 yards from where B Squadron worked on their tanks. The smell was terrible, and the Bosnians tried to drag as many people as they could into the cemetery to see the dead bodies. Thankfully we managed to avoid the invitation and after three days the bodies were reinterred.

Kljuc received more visits. We held a Warrant Officers and Sergeants Mess dinner night and General Jackson (Commander of the multi-national division we were a part of) appeared. The Canadians senior NCO's were in attendance. The Canadians were not supposed to drink at all. We managed to hide them from the Canadian Brigadier who arrived unexpectedly during the dinner. We also held games nights and took part in inter unit Rugby against the Canadians. Having lost the Rugby, the Canadians challenged us to street hockey. I very much regretted stating that Hockey was a game played by women when the Canadian Company Sergeant Major insisted I go in goal. The score was about 60 goals to nil and I was black and blue. The Canadian brief had been to show me what a girls game hockey was. They had long sticks, a very hard puck and a target, me.

At the end of spring General Dudakovic, who had commanded the Bosnian forces during the siege of Bihac appeared on the scene. He was unhappy that there were Croat forces in Kulen Vakuf, a town which straddled a river marking the border with Croatia. He threatened to bring his forces from Bihac and take matters into his own hands. The Battle Group could not allow that and therefore deployed our Challengers onto the one route he could take. It was a very tense situation for some time. General Walker, the NATO commander in the field at the time visited and snorted "Is this little place what it's all about?". General Jackson visited and talked with Dudakovic. Slowly it calmed down. The Croats moved into their correct positions and Dudakovic got back into his box.

As summer approached Corimecs appeared. These were container sized cabins for accommodation. In Kljuc they were stacked on top of each other due to the limited real estate. No sooner than they were installed and we moved in than we moved out as a Warrior recovery vehicle brake snapped and it rolled into the lower level. I was a little concerned that the Artificer Sergeant Major, despite 20+ years of experience on armoured vehicles had not worked out that you could not stop a rolling 30 ton Warrior by holding onto its tow hook.

T34 and Challenger at Kljuc.

CO, RSM and Martin Bell enjoying Bushmills in Mrkonjic Grad on St Patricks Day 1996.

THE SOLTAU FOX

Training during the height of the Cold War could be monotonous and dangerous, but at times very interesting. On 3 August 1959 the Federal Republic of Germany, Canada and the United Kingdom signed a special agreement in Bonn permitting exercises in the area of Soltau-Lüneburg in order to be able to train to defend Germany in the event of attack during the Cold War.

The agreement permitted stationed troops to conduct exercises all-year-round within the specified area. Villages and farmsteads were not to be used as military objectives and armoured vehicles could not move on Sundays or public holidays

During the early 70's such an exercise was undertaken by the QRIH and we were very good, however, after a regimental night march B Squadron had one tank unaccounted for and Sunday was fast approaching. The tank was 23Charlie, Commanded by Yorky Connolly, who due to his geographical awareness was known to all as the Soltau Fox. It was nearing midnight when the Squadron Leader Major Dick Webster, who in his youth had been the regimental heavy weight boxing champion and not known for taking prisoners, was quite relaxed about his missing tank. Having asked Yorky several times on the radio what is your ETA and having received, "Be with you in five minutes," for about an hour, decides Yorky is lost. Dick told him to halt his vehicle, look around, and then describe what he could see. Yorky's description placed him somewhere on the pylon line a well-known feature of the training area. The Squadron Leader said that was good as the Squadron hide was close to the pylon track. The Squadron Leader would switch on his searchlight and Yorkie could use that to make his way into the squadron hide. Yorky replied he couldn't see a light, the Squadron Leader with resignation in his voice said, "Look behind you." "Oh yes," said Yorky, "there it is." Major Webster then ordered him to head for the searchlight. "When you get into the Squadron hide, dismount, come to my tank, get on the turret where you will then climb up the searchlight beam and once you're at the *$%^?* F-in top I'll switch the bloody thing off....................you lunatic!"

Phil Nunn B Sqn Signal Sgt QRIH.

ARMAGH AND SOUTH ARMAGH – 1997

Shortly after the Guidon Parade in June 1997 the Regiment began training for a deployment on Op Banner to Northern Ireland. D and HQ Squadrons along with elements of RHQ would be in territory over which The Queens Own Hussars had operated during 1977 and they would again be operating out of Drumadd Barracks. C Squadron, under the Command of Major Tom Beckett would operate out of Keady and Middletown and B Squadron under Major Rob Hutton would operate out of Bessbrook Mill in South Armagh. Training was completed at Lydd and Hythe in Kent where there was another version of Tin City (the FIBUA village in Sennelager).

I had been a trooper in 1977 and a part of Recce Troop. As RSM on this tour I had a degree of freedom and was able to visit all the regimental locations. In 1997 I was amazed to see that a piece of carpet we had managed to scrounge in 1977 was still in the room we had put it in. Drumadd barracks had not changed a bit. The city of Armagh was pretty similar although the shops mirrored the shops in any British city at that time. Fewer small businesses and more supermarkets and charity shops.

B Squadron operated primarily in a surveillance role, manning a line of observation towers (the Romeo towers) perched on top of a number of hilltops. They were equipped with excellent observation equipment. Although not on the highest ground the tallest of the towers was Romeo 16 and overlooked the A1 and Newry. In anything other than a mild breeze the tower would sway. It could sway up to a metre or more and on many a night was more like a ship in a storm than a tower fixed to land. You needed a strong stomach when you were up in the tower. At the base of the tower was the accommodation area which was reasonably comfortable. It did however have the tallest toilet I have ever come across. When seated my feet were a foot off the floor.

B Squadron also patrolled Newry, Bessbrook and the surrounding areas. On one patrol a member of a team I was with suddenly announced that he had used to live "In that house there." Needless to say, he did not patrol that area again. All of the Squadron (and those in other locations) got acquainted with rural patrolling and that nightmare of all nightmares, the Blackthorn hedge!

At Christmas, one of the lads allowed me to lose my cool when, on returning from somewhere or other in a covert car I was greeted by the guard sitting in a chair wearing a Santa hat. The guard was surprised at my ranting at him but as he was manning the gate at which the last British soldier to die in the province had been shot I think I was justified. His face however just said "Really? Its Christmas!"

Keady and Middletown had often been mortared heavily in the past and the bases were now largely in bunker type buildings where the light of day did not shine. I went on a patrol with SSgt Knott and the indomitable Sgt Jones and was reminded that "Tea stops" existed and that people who got stroppy at having their car searched were dealt with fairly but robustly!

I was also able to visit the Infantry Company in Crossmaglen. This base had been attacked numerous times over the years, famously on one occasion with an improvised flamethrower. A farm slurry tanker was adapted to carry fuel and fire the lit fuel out of the drain nozzle. It was used to attack the main guard sanger, known as the Borucki sanger (reported on BBC news, you can still watch it on google). Amazingly, for the entire six months of a tour, this tower was manned by the same Infantry section. They knew everything that went on in their patch, who would wake at what time, who would go to work and when anything untoward happened they quickly picked up on it. The base of the tower was an enormous automated fire extinguisher. The sleeping accommodation was on the second level (a couple of beds and a cooker surrounding the hole in the floor used for access) and the top level was the observation platform. In my opinion those that manned the tower were a special breed (or completely cuckoo) as this was their world for six months.

The tour passed without major incident. The most dangerous moment was perhaps the catholic padre lighting candles during a service in Bessbrook mill. The candles were placed by some curtains that promptly went up and the attic chapel suffered some damage. The other night of real note was the evening of the Glasgow derby between Rangers and Celtic. B Squadron shared the mill with the Kings Own Scottish Borderers. Almost every Sgt in the battalion prowled the corridors of the mill that night (all night) ensuring that the two sets of supporters did not do more damage than the IRA!

For the Queens Royal Hussars this was a good tour. A good job had been done across all the regimental areas and there were no casualties. Time to return to Germany, catch up on courses and after only a short break get ready for the next tour, Kosovo.

A BROKEN HEARTED CLOWN – Names have been changed to protect the guilty!

This story finds the QRIH in Munster in the mid-80s. Where at the NAAFI bar Tpr Smith, Jack to his friends, is crying into his beer having received a Dear John letter from a local German girl. He was explaining to the new NAAFI manageress that he really needs to see this girl but has no transport. This conversation went on for most of the evening. The manageress wishing to close the bar foolishly gave Jack a bottle of spirits, which for whatever reason she could not sell. She then told him to go to bed and sleep on it. Never give a trooper a bottle of spirits and expect him to sleep on it, it's just not going to happen.

At about three in the morning the Guard Commander sitting at his post hears what he thinks is a tank starting up but that can't be? Then the engine noise gets louder and louder he goes outside the guardroom looks up the road in time to see a Chieftain, the main battle tank of the British Army screaming down towards the main gate in top gear. He looks across the road and sees a young inexperienced trooper on guard with his hand held high screaming at the top of his voice "HALT!"

In the middle of the main gates is a brand-new sentry box which the Quartermaster, Jim McLucas was extremely proud of. It had solar panels, the barriers were pushbutton, it kept you dry and out of the wind but above all it had a heater. The boys loved it. The Guard Commander explained "Sir I thought whoever was driving the tank must've known the boys loved that box because it looked like he was going to miss it, then for some inexplicable reason he flicked the tiller as he passed, and the arse of the tank screwed right and the sentry box was no more." The reminder of the Guard looked out of the top window in disbelief, the only thing they could make out was the red glow of the electric fire glinting through the dust of the totally flattened sentry box. The cry went up, "Where's Hammy?" (on Stag).

"I'm over here," came a squeaky voice trying to remove itself from a hedge. I'm told another member of the guard, which

I believe was Ginge Booth (Regimental goal keeper so a safe pair of hands) sprinted across the road and pulled the young trooper out the way just as the tank came flying past. The tank is now through the main gates out onto the main road, through the red traffic lights, hard left stick and is now heading for the city of Munster.

Almost immediately the RSM received a telephone call. In disbelief he says, "You're telling me someone has stolen one of our tanks?" "Yes," came the reply. In a cold voice, similar to that of Arnold Schwarzenegger he said, "I am on my way". On arrival he was briefed, and then accompanied by the Provost Sgt went around the barracks collecting evidence. He looked up and saw the lights were on in C squadron bar and thought, "if the beer taps are on, someone dies." As he entered the bar there was a shocked silence. He demanded to know what was going on. A JNCO giving him a slightly embarrassed look said "We're running a book sir, on how far the Chieftain will get before it breaks down". "Oh Indeed" said the RSM, "who's got the sweet bet." The JNCO said "Sergeant Stirling with 10 km." As the RSM was not sure if it was legal to place such bets on Her Majesty's equipment, he left them to it.

It transpires that as the tank disappeared from the barracks so did the Regimental Orderly Cpl (ROC) Owen McNeely, who grabbed the duty driver, his Land Rover and two escorts (with locked and loaded pick axe handles), Trooper's Mark Dornan and Phil Mitchel. They quickly caught up with the stolen vehicle and much to the ROC's relief and everyone else's the tank did not head for the city centre but turned onto the ring road. Of course, there was nothing he could do but follow it and hope Sgt Stirling's bet proved correct. This was not to be the case and the tank drove on through the night. With a rogue tank you immediately tell the civil as well as the military authorities, so the Polizei were also on the hunt. The tank made it to the small German village of Telgte, some 16km. This is your typically pretty German hamlet, cobbled streets; cars parked either side, not a lot of space in-between. Trooper Smith was clearly a bit of an expert. He put 55 tons through those streets and never lifted one cobblestone or damaged one car. He then brought the vehicle to a halt outside a closed nightclub. On moving to the front of the tank the ROC could see a very drunken trooper trying to exit. Putting his hand on the troopers shoulder and recognising the culprit he said "Smith, you're nicked!" to which Jack replied, "No not yet I've got to get to the nightclub and speak to my girlfriend." The ROC replied, "Jack it's been closed for hours." Jack burst into tears.

At that moment two German police cars with sirens blaring and lights flashing came screaming round the corner. The ROC described it later thus. "He got out the car and just kept growing and growing. He must've been about 8 foot tall. He had a slashed peak cap and was immaculate from head to foot. He strode purposely towards the front of the tank and with a trembling arm pointed to the cupola and in a deep voice demanded to know "Wo is die Blinklicht?" (Where is the flashing light?). The ROC at a loss for words gave him the telephone number of the Orderly Officer. (Good move son.)

The following day Jack is marched in front of the Adjutant who is trying to put together the whole sorry tale. Captain Nigel Hill, a really good egg says, "Right Smith. I think I understand it all and how things progressed but there's one thing I can't quite understand and that is why you got changed into uniform before you stole the tank?" With a look of stunned disbelief Smith said, "Sir you know as well as I do, you cannot drive a military vehicle in civilian clothes". Smith went back to the nick.

I don't believe he ever got to see his girlfriend as not long afterwards he was given a corrective period in Colchester. It is nice to imagine that someone may have sneaked her into his cell but life ain't like that.

After note: You would expect Divisional Headquarters to have a reasonable working knowledge of the vehicles under their command. Their most pressing question, for which they demanded an immediate answer, was "How did he get the ignition keys?!"

Phil Nunn RSM, QRIH. I was there!

MORE DOORS OPEN IN MUNSTER

I liked Smith. Not only was he an excellent tank driver but had we been at war he would have won medals. He was again in nick, this time with another prisoner by the name of Seamus, both serving time for GBH. They had noticed no one checked the locked empty cell directly across the corridor, the one attached to the outer wall of the Guardroom. The pair then learnt they could open it using the butter knife one of them had kept when told to make tea for the Provo Staff. Seamus persuaded his girlfriend to smuggle them in a hacksaw blade during one of her prison visits and for almost a week they slowly cut through the bars of the empty cell. Each night before they finished they would cover their work by rubbing boot polish into the cuts. When the night of the Great Escape arrived, they waited for the optimum moment and entered the empty cell. With a few strong strokes of the saw blade all the bars came away. They clambered through the window then jumped over the outside wall by the side of the Toc H cafe. Now out on the street and dressed in the civvies which they had managed to secrete away, they collected themselves and made good their escape. They did however leave a note on Smiths' bed which read "It is the right and duty of every prisoner to escape; which we have done so tonight, love and kisses Jack and Seamus." Every great escape has a purpose. Theirs was not to run away but to go for a beer, so they quickly made their way to a local bar. Several hours later when the barman realised they could not pay the bill he rang the RMP who returned them to the nick. As Seamus said later, "Well, it saved us paying for a taxi."

We should have realised earlier that Smith would always have a problem when it comes to personal transportation.

There were a few demotions that month...........all part of the rough filter we call military discipline

Phil Nunn MTO QRIH

IRAQ - OP TELIC 8 - 2006

The Regiment had been on tour in Iraq prior to OP Telic 8 but as this is not a history and as I was away on a posting it is not included here. It was however a very good tour with its fair share of action resulting in a Military Cross for one member of the Regiment and several other awards. The fact that it is not mentioned in this book does not lessen its significance and I am sure it is covered in the full Regimental history.

Some of the story of Op Telic 8 is in the training required for it. The complexity of modern tours demands skills ranging from normal armoured Battle Group drills, search, learning the culture of the locals in whose area you will operate, theatre specific kit training (learning all about Mastiff, Bulldog, Warrior etc), and FIBUA (Fighting in Built Up Areas). Some of those that deployed on Telic 8 had spent a total of 245 days in the 12 months prior to deployment on various training courses and exercises and were exhausted at the beginning of the tour!

Having taken over HQ Squadron in 2004 training proper for Telic 8 began in 2005. Before that the Squadron had deployed to Hohne Ranges for some low level training and I worked to build the manpower strength up to its full requirement. I don't think I will upset any of my previous colleagues when I say that parts of HQ Squadron had for many years been the repository for those that might not have found working on tanks to their liking. With the agreement of the CO the sabre squadrons were told to cough up some of their manpower to make up the shortfall in HQ. This was the opportunity for the sabre squadron leaders to move some of their less enthusiastic members on, or so they thought.

The days of chucking anyone into HQ Squadron and telling them to drive and operate a fuel truck or run highly complex accounts are long gone. By 2004 MT drivers had to hold numerous qualifications and be trained in seven modules of Hazardous Materials handling, all of which required lengthy courses. Paper accounting was on the way out and computers were very definitely on the way in. In short, the guys that came into HQ had to be up to speed. When it was clear that some of those being sent were possibly not suited to HQ I sent them back and told the relevant squadron to provide AN Other. I think this was probably the first time this had been done and it needed the full support of the CO and 2IC as the Sabre Squadron commanders were not happy at having to give up some of their better men. Some really good lads came into HQ Squadron and their skillsets and attitudes rubbed off on those who had been in the Squadron for a long time. All this did not mean that some of those in the Squadron were not some of the least fit in the Regiment!

One of the Squadrons first training events was held on Hohne ranges. MT and those that could be spared from the QM and QM tech departments deployed. One of the assets that tank soldiers rarely see at Hohne is a FIBUA village. It is not quite as big as Imber village or Copehill Down (both on Salisbury Plain) nor as complex as Tin City in Sennelager, but we could develop some of the Infantry skills that might be required. Recce Troop acted as the enemy. The plan was to move into an Assembly Area and then a Forming Up Point just short of the village. This was to be done by foot at night and then we would attack at first light, let off lots of pyrotechnics, move from one end of the village to the other practicing various building entry drills and then endex. That was the plan anyway.

On the evening we had planned to move to the Assembly Area all the members of MT and the stores troops and several clerks lined up and began the foot move, about four miles. For many of HQ Squadron this was challenging territory! Carrying a weapon correctly and moving with the correct spacing between each other was almost beyond some but then it got a whole lot more adventurous. The heavens opened and a real Hohne fog set in. Having spent 28 years in Germany I had never seen rain like it and the fog meant you could just see your hand in front of your face. Thankfully everyone was by now issued really good goretex waterproofs. I had also been out during the previous day and marked the route with Cyalumes pushed into the ground, so I could keep on track and look as if I could map read. When we got into the assembly area the rain was still coming down like the monsoon and the feet of everyone were soaked so I told them all to change into dry socks. It became clear that to some, the carrying of spare socks or even Goretex was not common practice and several had to be pulled off the exercise to avoid hypothermia. Lesson learned.

The move from the Assembly Area to the Forming Up Point went well. The attack started, and the rain stopped. At the first house a ladder was brought up and placed against a first floor window. A member of the squadron climbed the ladder. He was one of the larger members of the squadron. He could not fit through the window and attempted to reverse. The ladder snapped. We threw him through a much larger ground floor window.

Recce troop had done a pretty good job of finding thorn bushes to pack up all the stair wells. The QM Tech (Joe Mercer), I and the Detachment Commander (2IC of clerks) shouted encouragement and threw pyrotechnics. The Detachment Commander was a young officer (see article on Ruperts) and tried to steal the pyrotechnics but on finding he was watched threw them and added to the general chaos. A couple of the lads got punchy with each other and had to be calmed down. Eventually the attack succeeded, every building had been cleared and everyone was completely knackered. I doubt very much that we had improved our Infantry skills, but we had all had a ball and for HQ Squadron this was a new and team building experience. One or two of the Squadron had done nothing like it since their basic training.

More training took place in camp and lecture followed lecture. Vulnerable point drills, vehicle ambush drills, IED drills, all came thick and fast. We learned that a lot of the SCOTS DG Battle Group were going down with a vomiting bug and diarrhoea. I told the Squadron only those that were gungy and too lazy to wash their hands got it. I got it after two weeks in theatre. Another lesson learned.

Battle Group training took place in Poland on a training area called Drasko Pomorskie. Smaller than BATUS it is never the less a big training area. Used in the past by Soviet forces it did have a fair bit of ordnance lying about so you had to take care. Our Battle Group consisted of a Company of Light Infantry and a

Company of PWRR, the same company from whom the last British soldier to win a VC came from (in the same area we were to deploy to, Al Amarah). Training passed off fairly uneventfully save for two incidents. In the first I was out conducting a recce (fishing!) when I happened across a very drunken polish male. He stopped me and told me I could have sex with the equally drunken polish female he was with for 10 Euro's. Getting him to go away was not easy so discretion became the better half of valour and we looked elsewhere. I am glad that Battle group training that day was in a different area. The female was a bit like Medusa and would have turned many of the battle group off women for a very long time!

The second incident was a Battle Group drill. One of the harder things to organise is a Battle Group replenishment (replen). It is a complex operation and takes time to set up in order to feed sub units through the replenishment system in the fastest possible time. The one thing that can balls up this complex operation is the Infantry and true to form the Light Infantry Company in their Warriors came from the wrong direction and came head on with the PWRR company. Warrior APCs ended up mixed in with the wrong company going to the wrong places. I was later told that I swore on the radio (a lot) and that this was bad and that I should control my voice procedure. By last light however everyone had been through the replen and were with their correct sub units.

By the time it came to go on a Recce to Iraq the Squadron was well drilled and could handle anything thrown at them. We boarded a Tristar to Basra airfield. Landing at night we were told to put on body armour and helmets on the approach. All lights went out and then the aircraft went into what can only be described as a vertical dive. My stomach was about three feet behind the rest of me and the look of terror on the Brigade officers face in the next seat to mine must have mirrored my own. I think at least one helmet was filled as we landed without being shot out of the sky. Shortly after that it was into a Hercules and those going to Al Amarah landed at a desert airstrip called Sparrow Hawk. From there we were loaded into Saxon armoured vehicles and taken into Camp Abu Naji, the then home of the SCOTS DG Battle Group.

We saw all that Abu Naji had to offer which, apart from accommodation and food was not much. The camp boundaries were marked by a large earthen berm with fortified fighting positions built into it. Many of the troops slept in Rubb shelters (large semi tubular tents with plastic flooring. Much better than the 18x24' tentage we had used on previous tours). The majority of the tented accommodation was being removed as the number of troops in the camp was to be reduced. That left most accommodated in portacabin type buildings with about ten to a hut. We attended the Battle Group briefing and found ourselves under our first rocket attack. Most of the time the "incoming" were 107mm rockets. Very basic. Lay a piece of angle iron on the ground, put the rocket on the angle iron and light the blue touch paper sort of stuff. Provided you had got the angle of flight right and had set up a launch site at roughly the distance the rockets could fly you had a reasonable chance of the rocket landing in the camp. Those that did land in camp had a 60/40 chance of going off and when they did they could cause real damage. There were many stories of near misses and sadly there had been casualties in the past.

The Warriors and tanks were all covered in bar armour (like large metal fences around the vehicle). The aim of the bar armour was to stop Rocket propelled grenades (RPG) from impacting against the vehicles and it was very effective. On several occasions the bomb disposal team had to be called out to make safe rounds stuck in the bar armour of vehicles returning from patrol in Al Amarah.

After a couple of days, it was time to leave and get back to training in Germany where it was late winter and very cold. "Paddies Day" arrived. If you are a squadron leader "Paddies Day" (St Patricks Day, March 17th) is not something you look forward to. The day kicks off with "Gunfire" for the soldiers (being woken up and offered copious amounts of Blackbush Whiskey) and then the bed race takes place. This involves the Squadron Leaders being carried for a distance and then thrown onto some cobbled together trolley and run around a course around the camp. Those carrying you are members of your squadron. Everyone else in the camp is trying to kill you. Once the race starts members of other squadrons try to scotch your attempt to complete the course. This usually involves throwing very heavy items (skips, track links, oil cans etc) at the "bed" and its occupant and trying to thin the carrying team out using fire hoses, tripping them up or just hijacking them by force of numbers. Other members of your squadron are of course trying to prevent this whilst trying to kill the other squadron leaders! Complete chaos, black and blue by the end of it but great fun. There is then a parade of sorts and Shamrock is presented. As with all traditions there is a purpose. It bonds people and helps to form esprit de corps.

Training finished it was time to deploy. Movement Control Check Points (MCCP - still!), coach rides to airports and flights out. We travelled into a country to the south of Iraq and then boarded Hercules for the flights in to Basra. From there flights departed to Sparrow Hawk (the desert airstrip close to Al Amarah) for QRH Battle Group personnel and we began the business of relieving SCOTS DG. The CO (Lt Col Labouchere) eventually took over and assumed control for the Battle Group goat!

We had a number of issues. The first of these was that the support weapons of the company coming to us from the Light Infantry had been taken off them and issued to the members of QRH joining the Infantry Battle Group, leaving us without enough Minimi sub machine guns and 40mm Under slung grenade launchers (UGL). The SA 80 in the light support weapon role is a pretty decent affair but does not have the punch of the Minimi which was far better for the role we were in. Secondly soldiers were going down with Diarrhoea and Vomiting (D+V) at an alarming rate. The fact that I went down with it within a couple of weeks of arriving having told my squadron only gungy people got it did not mean that there was little sympathy for me. Completely the contrary and music was even played on BFBS radio for me. Johnny Cash I think it was, Burning Ring of Fire. Great! The cause of this outbreak was not a failure to wash as I found out. Lavatory facilities in Abu Naji were portaloos. 41 of them to be precise for up to 1400 soldiers. The contents of these were sucked out on a daily basis by a truck manned by two locals. The "Shit sucker" could not go too far from camp (as it was an easy target) so it drove off a few hundred yards and then "Dumped" (I like that pun) its contents into a large pit. This dried, turned to dust and was then blown back over the camp. Nice.

The saga of the support weapons went on for some time but eventually it was agreed that they would be flown into Sparrowhawk on one of the supply flights that took place. On the given night I was waiting like an expectant father for my babies (Minimi MGs and UGL) to arrive. Sure enough, three large cardboard boxes arrived. Swiss pen knife out, black tape cut and three boxes of brand new Wellington boots. In the desert, in summer. I must have felt a little like the Para's at Arnhem who wanted ammunition and got berets. After a short phone call to brigade staff the weapons arrived a couple of nights later.

The heat inside armoured vehicles during the day was intense. Air temperatures were at about the 40 degree mark, sometimes a lot hotter. Inside the vehicles it was getting on for 70 – 80 degrees (that's about what you get when you open an oven I have been told). Having plenty of water in the vehicles was essential. One individual could easily drink thee litres during a patrol. On one trip out (for the life of me I cannot remember why I had gone out) I was in a Saxon armoured personnel carrier with one of my more rotund Motor Transport troop members commanding the vehicle. Because of the threat only the Commanders hatch was open. This lad was big. Very round. He formed a perfect seal about the one open hatch and no air was getting into the vehicle. We looked for the water of which there were only two bottles and that went in minutes. Body armour was taken off. Helmets were taken off. We pulled on the trouser legs of the large round TA lad but to no avail. Eventually we arrived back in camp. One soldier had fainted and I would of as well had we been in the vehicle for another couple of minutes. The large TA lad said "What?" at the looks he was being given. Lessons learned. Check water. Sack fat lad!

On May 5th Abu Naji was hit by a completely different type of attack. Fifty five rounds of pretty accurate 120mm mortar landed in camp in the space of ten minutes. Most of us were completely unphased by 107mm rockets and stayed in bed when the warbling alarm sounded. I got out of bed pretty bloody quickly when the first 120mm round exploded. Very different and not too far away from me. Very unsocial! The attack is reputed to have been the heaviest mortar/ artillery attack against the British Army since the Korean war. It may well have been. I just lay under my bed listening to rounds going off in the vicinity and it was plenty big enough for me!

The Infantry company thoroughly enjoyed the attack! They took cover quickly and watched one end of a cabin being hit and blown to pieces. From the other end at a rate of knots emerged a young female Gunner Lieutenant. Her speed of exit had dictated her dress. Helmet, tick! Body armour, tick! Light blue knickers big tick! Nothing else. The boys loved it with many of them shouting, "Bring it on!"

Despite the amount of tented accommodation being reduced numbers had remained fairly constant and soldiers were pretty well crammed into anywhere they could fit a bed in. The Infantry company told me they needed 30000 more sandbags to properly protect themselves in the event of another attack. I requested them. 90 rotting bags that were no good to man nor beast arrived. Unbelievable!

News came that the camp would close, and the Battle Group would become mobile in the desert in a role of "Overwatch". As plans were made to dismantle the camp and get the stores back to Basra I had to leave the organisation of this mammoth task to the two Regimental Quarter Master Sergeants and a young LE Captain as I was now to be posted to Cyprus. HQ Squadron, to a man, did a sterling job throughout the tour and supported the Battle Group magnificently.

AN EYE OPENER

Attending the Drill Course was amusing for many reasons and to a Cavalry soldier even more so. All students SNCO's were treated like young guardsmen throughout the course. In essence you had to adapt quickly and accept the pettiness of the punishments with a smile. I remember on my second morning parading by my bed. Immaculate I thought, but not the case said the Drill Sergeant. My alarm clock showed the right time, 0750, but because it showed the wrong time I was to parade behind the guard at 1800hrs. The Drill Sergeant could see I was confused and proceed to enlighten me. If my Alarm clock was to be on display it was to show the proper time 1231. '1231' said I? Yes said the Drill Sergeant in his parade ground voice ONE.......TWO THREE.......ONE. However, we had the last laugh. Sgt Jones, a Brummie with an excellent sense of humour, was not to be out done. On one of the last Room Inspections the Depot RSM, in NO1 Dress and white gloves, carried out the Inspection. When he came to Sgt Jones he looked him up and down before moving behind him and running his gloved finger along the window ledge. Returning to stand in front of Sgt Jones he showed him the immaculate gloved finger was now black with dust. 'Explain Sgt Jones' he bawled. 'My Window Box Sir'. Never has a room laughed so silently!!

TROOP LEADER MEMORIES

Sam Hatlem-Olsen

"Did you enjoy the Army?" is a frequently asked question in civilian life. My answer is always the same. "Yes, the parties were great."

Flippant, perhaps; true, for sure. But not, of course, the whole story. There was so much more to being a Troop Leader. It is some of the finest training for the future that a young man can receive, a hothouse without parallel for learning about both life and self.

Life lessons started with the soldiers. For someone from a homely, middle class, public school environment in rural Leicestershire, meeting and getting to know the Troop was as revelatory as anything before or since. Tales of youth spent on the Shankill, or in Yardley Wood, or on the Jamaican sugar plantations, was to be exposed to ways of life that I hadn't come close to touching before. I appreciate the country in a way that none of my non-military contemporaries could possibly do.

There was the foreign experience too. Tours to Kosovo and Iraq opened our eyes, both to alien cultures, but also to the inadequacies of political support for our Army. The Government's allocation of funds to prepare us for war, for a northern invasion of Iraq that thankfully never came, was scandalously short to say the least. No wonder the likes of Johnny Mercer MP make their way into Parliament, changing the system from within.

Then there was, of course, the fun. I had enjoyed a party or two at university, but Army soirees took enjoyment to a new level, especially as Mess Silver Member. Take the summer ball; the feeling is hard to describe, but a charged wave of expectation flows from the tips of my shoulder blades and down into my stomach when I recall the first roll of drums as the band marched in.

...Ah, at last, and here they come now: Sgt Edwards, with Troopers Robb and Chapman, and of course Corporal Findlay leading the bagpipe charge...

We felt each other tapping along, loudly of course, to make sure our fellow Troop Leaders knew we were wrapping ourselves in the Regiment's culture, but also to impress the girls we had invited along.

Yet the fun, as anyone who served will admit, didn't just revolve around balls and dinner nights. There was also the continuous banter and japes.

'Ridiculous', says my early-middle-age self, what on earth was I doing cycling down the Mess corridor, at full pelt, towards Captain Steel with a pig stick in my hand? The two bottles of wine had moved me from a state of Dutch courage to one of reckless-ness, but still we charged. Neither of us managed a blow, thank goodness, otherwise I would have ended up like my Grandfather, hospitalised by a heady concoction of drink, exuberance, and being pierced through the side by a Mess sword. At least I had the excuse of youthfulness; he was a full Colonel.

The calculation – a mostly subconscious one, it must be accepted, especially at that age – was that this was the horseplay that would make us better, braver, leaders on the battlefield.

Becoming more courageous wasn't the only benefit of being a Troop Leader. It was also a good way to better understand yourself and how others see you. Let's face it, there's nowhere really to hide in the Regiment, especially on operations, and the Troop and Squadron NCOs were quick to point out shortcomings that needed to be rectified.

I once returned from a patrol in Kosovo, in the late autumn of 2000, to be greeted by a stern looking Regimental Sergeant Major, John Nutt. My Troop Sergeant, Steve Milliken, was not happy with me. RSM Nutt and I went to the briefing room with a cup of tea and sat down opposite each other on the black plastic chairs. I removed my swept-back-style beret and placed it next to my mug and fidgeted with a pen. I knew it was not going to be an easy chat.

'The thing is, Mr H-O, he's never had a Troop Leader like you,' said the RSM. 'To be blunt, you're too hands on, and you sometimes do the wrong thing in front of the Squadron. Some people are saying you can't take advice. I think they're wrong, are they?'

If I couldn't take advice before, I could now. It's never easy to learn that you're doing things the wrong way, but if you are keen to listen and improve then being a Troop Leader can be the making of you.

Learning your own limits started at Sandhurst. The log races, the assault courses, the endless drill; all showed how you could push yourself to spaces neither your soul nor mind could have imagined. It was only as a Troop Leader though that the boundaries were pushed furthest. The responsibility of looking after three tanks and eleven men drove me on, drove us all on, ably and fiercely supported by the Troop Sergeants and Corporals who were unlucky enough to find themselves with us.

Looking back, being a Troop Leader has crafted my character more than any other influence. Whether it is in the understanding of my fellow man, being aware of how others judge you, or being able to keep going whatever the challenge, all were fired in the Athlone furnace. I can also drink five pints from a didgeridoo and fit in a fridge, but these skills haven't been so useful, sadly.

Every generation thinks that it is the pinnacle, and what comes behind a pale imitation. As the Roman poet Horace wrote, we all believe the youth to be "a Progeny Yet More Corrupt".

Yet if the current and future romp of Troop Leaders can take the opportunities to improve themselves presented by their role, whilst serving the Regiment and Country in the most superlative of fashion, then they will make themselves equal, or even surpass, the men that went before them.

THE OFFICERS MESS – THE LIFE OF RUPERT

Not by David Attenborough

A Rupert is the name given to a young man (or lady or gender free entity) who for reasons beyond comprehension believes that he/she will survive several years as a young Army Officer unscathed before leaving the Army to work somewhere in the city. Ruperts are also referred to as Rodney's (of Del Boy fame) as they usually display no common sense and follow troop sergeants like puppies. The dog in the film "UP" could have been called a Rodney (or Rupert)! For the purposes of this article Ruperts will be male.

A Rupert does not start life in the same way as a normal person. They are created by the dreams of their parents and grandparents. Somewhere in their past is a military success story and their parents have tried to clone them. Ruperts are not born with an alcohol gene.

At a young age the Rupert is sent to a very expensive boarding school. Sometimes these schools, such as Eton are booked many years before the Rupert is actually born and on very rare occasions even before his parents are! This assumes that the mother and father of the Rupert get their timing correct to a nanosecond and that the Rupert tadpole is a strong swimmer. Letters may be sent to regimental secretaries requesting interviews with regimental Colonels on such and such a date in twenty years when, "Rupert will by then have gained a first in Romano Greek history (never anything useful – not good form!) and be ready for some action!" All this takes planning. Ruperts are not born with the planning gene.

At some stage in their early twenties Ruperts travel to Westbury to test their suitability for the life ahead. They and others are given a plank and a couple of barrels and told to cross a river or build a city. The Rupert that can persuade all other Ruperts in the group that he is right wins a ticket to Sandhurst and may even become a potential Cavalry Officer.

Whilst in Sandhurst the Rupert is broken and then rebuilt. He learns self-respect, planning and is pushed to his limits. Surprisingly when push comes to shove these limits often exceed those of a normal soldier, but the Rupert is usually unaware of that. He learns etiquette, and how to behave in front of senior Officers. He learns how to leap tall buildings and throw himself off the same. He learns to tell the truth. In his final term an alcohol gene is inserted. After many months (a year) of being shouted at he can iron a shirt and march (after a fashion) and he is allowed to take part in the "Sovereigns Parade". It is unfortunately a sad fact that a memory gene is not inserted at the same time as the alcohol gene because excessive testing of the alcohol gene over the fortnights leave following attendance at Sandhurst completely erases all memories of any subject taught.

On arriving at the Regiment, the Rupert earns another title. He becomes a "Subby". The Subby is given a troop of soldiers to command. They call him a Rupert or a Rodney in discussion between themselves. To his face he is "Sir" if he is an officious little git or "Boss" if the troop like him. His alcohol gene is far more likely to be exercised by the soldiers if he is known as "Boss". In the evenings he returns to being a Subby and is fair game for any senior subby or Captain. In one Officers mess that had two corridors the subbies had one corridor and the Captains the other. Subbies would run down their corridor trying to avoid appearing at the windows whilst the Captains would shoot at them with shotguns or flares. This practice was halted when one of the subbies was wounded.

When subbies experience alcohol they mentally press self-destruct buttons and see how many extra duties they can accrue in the shortest space of time possible. The destruct phase begins in the mess. Champagne is opened, usually with no regard to where the missile of a cork may go resulting in several injuries and significant repair costs. If the Rupert is particularly macho, he opens the Champagne with a sword. If this is successful other Ruperts may be impressed. If it fails, the wrist of the Rupert that attempted to open the bottle is badly lacerated and the other Ruperts are really impressed and try it themselves. This leads to a blood letting not seen since the 300 defeated the Persians. After only a few bottles and the introduction of a game called Cubuddy (which involves a burnt cork) Champagne is discarded, the Whiskey cudgel is taken up and more physical games follow. These may include tunnel rugby. Two sofas are turned upside down and thrown together forming a tunnel through which a team must pass whilst being assaulted by another team trying to go the other way. There are no rules and the odd eyeball hanging out of a socket is not uncommon. Black eyes are good form. Other games may include para rolling through mess windows, skateboarding in bare feet without a skateboard to see how much skin can be removed, or back sliding down the dining room table whilst compatriots try to fill you with Whiskey whilst you move. Other compatriots launch you (it cannot be termed a push) on your way as fast as they can so that you have no chance of breaking your fall when you come off the far end of the table. This has the beneficial effect of polishing the table. Fire jumping, handstand champagne drinking and seeing who can fit into a small fridge without breaking their back are all popular pastimes.

Then, of course there are the games that involve pyrotechnics. Pyrotechnics are fireworks, only bigger and far more lethal. They are issued to troops on exercise for battle simulation. Smoke grenades, shermuly parachute flares, thunderflashes (large bangers that can easily remove hands) and mini flares are the usual pyrotechnics issued. The role of the Subby is to steal pyrotechnics and hide them in their rooms in the mess. They then attempt to destroy either themselves, or the mess once the alcohol gene comes alive. One particularly successful recent attempt on an Officers mess occurred in Allenby barracks in Bovington courtesy of an Officer who was showing young subbies how to destroy things and used the Bovington Officers mess as a visual aid, destroying the top four floors of the building with a naval flare. Completely accidental. Good tricks include waiting until a fellow subby is asleep and then dropping a thunderflash into his room. The thunderflash may be inserted into a paint tin for greater effect as this will rapidly redecorate the room. If the colleague is less popular then a smoke grenade is thrown into the room. This has the effects of redecorating the room (and occupants) due to smoke damage (usually a dirty orange or yellow), choking the poor sleeping subby almost to death (particularly when all exits are deliberately blocked) and severely pissing off the Quarter Master who must then try and make good the damage without letting on what caused it. Thunderflashes may also be lowered on string from balconies so that they explode behind high ranking officers during visits. On the extra duties scale this is a huge hit.

If the subby is still alive after manic games and blowing everyone up he will usually get extra duties. These duties are awarded by an Adjutant, a very senior and usually grumpy Captain. Being on duty involves remaining sober and ensuring that there is an initial point of command should anything untoward such as injury or terrorist attack take place. If you recall, Rupert was not issued a memory gene immediately after leaving Sandhurst so the Adjutants instruction of "You may not drink" passes through a void. As soon as he can the subby presses the self destruct button and opens yet another bottle of Champagne. Now however, as someone whose alcohol gene is hardened, he is still able to attend such important events as guard mounting (the time at which those soldiers chosen to guard a barracks are paraded to ensure they are correctly equipped and alert). Unfortunately, the lack of a memory gene means that he arrives by bicycle wearing his dress hat, white gloves, George boots and nothing else. This is probably one of the largest of the hits on the extra duties scale.

Captains are subbies that have grown up. They invite attractive single people to parties in a vain attempt to hold off the effects of Champagne as they have all had lots of extra duties and have been blown up on numerous occasions. They instruct their female guests to show as much breast as possible as this is another trigger for subbies to attack champagne. Once the subby is being controlled by his alcohol gene they can wind them up mercilessly and tell the subby who to blow up.

A dinner night is an occasion when all the Officers in a Regiment have a formal evening. Mess dress is worn, and all are on their best behaviour as the Commanding Officer and ladies (wives of more senior officers) are in attendance. After some initial small talk and a couple of glasses of wine/whiskey/beer all the Officers and their guests make their way into the dining room and sit on either side of a long table. Waiters serve wine and food. Subbies, who invariably begin the small talk and couple of glasses phase of the night at about noon, then try and burble to the guest next to them. If the guest responds positively they behave reasonably well. If the guest does not respond or is aloof the subby will drink himself into a semi conscious state as quickly as possible. He will then slide under the table and attempt to get to a lady of his choice at the far end of the table whilst carrying a glass of wine and simultaneously attempting to steal the spurs from fellow Officers (spurs clip into mess dress boots). The response to this is a mass kicking from all males sitting at the table. Female subbies who attempt the feat are also open to getting a kicking and losing teeth but that is equal opportunities for you. Once the meal is finished music is played and all leave the dining room. Officers, regardless of rank, then switch on their alcohol genes and play the silly games alluded to earlier in this expose whilst their guests form small groups and wonder why they liked/ married the Officer who is now ignoring them and whom they will have to drive home and clean up later.

There is one type of officer who is usually able to understand and control his alcohol gene. This is the LE or Late Entry Officer. These are the grumpy old men that have been through the ranks and whose alcohol gene is expired. If, and it is a very big if, one of them collapses from the effects of alcohol he is fair game for whatever photographs can be taken of him (however they are staged) whilst he is comatose. The punishment for such an event is far worse than extra duties because such officers usually have equally grumpy and senior wives. One LE Officer was picked up by his wife at eight in the morning following a mess dinner. The fact that he was covered in shaving foam and barely conscious gave the game away. There was a black cloud in the car as he was driven from camp. Some eight hours later he was called and asked if his wife was talking to him. "Talking to me???? She has'nt stopped talking AT me!" was the reply.

LIFE AS A TROOP SERGEANT 2007-2008

Captain Neil Rudd

My time as a Sabre Troop Sergeant spanned from September 2007 through to October 2008. Prior to this I had spent the majority of my time in the QRH as part of Recce Tp, only working on CR2 to complete my conversion courses from Challenger and to complete my CR2 Gunnery Instructors in 2003. The two years prior to taking up the post of Tp Sgt were spent as an Army recruiting Sgt in the Army Careers Information Office Worcester, a post I thoroughly enjoyed. As it turned out I would meet a few of my applicants at Regimental Duty not long after returning to the Regiment!

So, having spent the previous ten years of my career on CVR(T) it was now time to try my hand at commanding a CR2 and being a troop sergeant and it was decided that that would be as 1st troop sergeant in A Squadron. The OC at the time was Major Jamie Howard and the SSM was WO2 Darrell Jones, two people I knew very well from my time in C Squadron as part of our Northern Ireland tour together. The Squadron was in good shape having returned from operations as part of Op Telic 8 at the start of the year and we were entering a training year prior to going to BATUS the following year and another deployment to Iraq at the end of 2008.

When I arrived a few of the guys were away on adventure training, but on the Monday morning we all got together in the troop store so that I could get to meet those that were there. Over a brew we all did a round of introductions for my benefit so that I could get a feel for the guys that I would be working with, Jellyhead, Dinger, Fudgepacker and Fish to name a few. I knew straight away that the troop had a few characters (more details as we go) and it was going to be good spending time with them. I also told the guys a little bit about myself, what I expected from them and that I was looking forward to being their troop sergeant.

One of the first responsibilities was to sign for the three CR2 for which I was going to be responsible and that meant only one thing, the CES check (a check of all tools and equipment on the vehicles, everyone's favourite). After Naafi break the guys got all of the kit out of the troop cages and laid it out next to their respective tanks. Whilst they were doing that I took the opportunity to sit down with the Troop Leader and Sergeant in the troop store to have a chat about the boys and learn a little more about what was coming up in the coming weeks and months. I had never met or worked with Rob Hammond or Fish previously, so it was also good to get a feel for them. With the CES now laid out Fish and I went to start the check, Rob Hammond, the Troop Leader did what troop leaders do best, left us to it and went back to his room. It seemed that the troop was in pretty good shape with only a few small items missing which had already been demanded. Knowledge of the various CES items was limited in some cases. Whilst going through the various spanners and checking them, "Jellyhead" got a little bit lost with the ring and open spanners. I had just called 10-11mm, 11mm ring and open and 13mm ring and open. He then asked, "was that 11-13mm ring and open?" After a few laughs from the others I pointed out that there was obviously no such spanner as a ring and open could only be one size, either 11 or 13mm. Jellyhead was certainly living up to his name in those first few hours.

One of the major systems which had been implemented on the tank park (and indeed across the Army) during my time away was the Joint Asset Management Equipment System (JAMES). It was a system now used to record all information about our vehicles such as, serial numbers, servicing, faults, repairs and demands. JAMES was designed to make accounting "easier" and reduce the need for as paperwork to be produced and eventually we would get rid of our vehicle documents and it would all be done electronically (10 years further down the line and we are still using just as much paperwork).

The first major training event that I was to deploy on with the troop would be Collective Training Level 1 (CT1) out on the local training areas of Sennelager. As always seems to be the case when deploying on exercise in Germany we would be training at the end of November in to early December, which resulted in fairly cold temperatures. For 1st troop the exercise was an overall success.

Between the Tp Ldr, Tp Cpl and I we ensured that the guys were well briefed on what we would be doing at each stage of the exercise and carried out rehearsals when required for the various phases we moved through. This paid particular dividends the night the OC decided to have each of the troop locations bumped. Our stand to positions reacted as they should and we collapsed our position, moving via the Emergency RV without incident and re-established in a new location within 90 mins. The other three troops did not react so well and as a result the OC ensured that they did not get much more sleep that night.

The highlight of the week however had nothing to do with our training. For the first time ever CR2 and the Sennelager training area would be the backdrop for a wedding! Trooper Ryan Packer and his fiancee were due to be married and were going to have a small affair at the Paderborn registry office, however the OC managed to convince them that it would be a great idea to have their wedding in front of two CR2 with their barrels crossed and witnessed by the whole squadron. So, just before 1000 on the last day of our exercise, we lined up the vehicles and awaited the arrival of the bride and our Padre who would conduct the service. Mrs Packer arrived right on time and was initially regretting the decision she had made as she emerged from the car wearing an Army issue softie jacket over her wedding dress to keep her warm in the sub-zero temperatures! The wedding service was short and sweet and the Squadron relished the opportunity to belt out a few hymns under the direction of the Padre. With the wedding complete it was time to get back to camp give the vehicles a quick check over and then get into the NAAFI bar to celebrate with the happy couple. By way of a thank you to the Squadron, Trooper Packer signed off the next week!!!

Our deployment to BATUS in Canada was in May for the first exercise of the season. I was fortunate enough to be selected to go out early as the Troop Sergeant for the activation of the Squadrons tanks in early April. I headed up a small team of SMEs (Subject Matter Experts) who went out to BATUS early to find out what the state of the CR2 fleet was and to conduct necessary maintenance. In typical Canada tradition we experienced all weather types in a 24hr period from sun, to rain, hail and snow and back again on more than one occasion. The workload was considerable. However, we did get a bit of time off too and the guys made the most of the opportunities to head off to Calgary and Edmonton.

When the rest of the Squadron arrived a few weeks later the vehicles were at a good base standard for the troops to come and carry out the rest of the maintenance. Before we knew it, D Day arrived, and we were ready for the off. The OPFOR (for the old and bold for who remember only live fire that is Opposition force using simulator equipment) that year was led by some of our own Regiment and a former RSM who was now an LE had taken the opportunity to wind up the Squadron before we had even left camp. We arrived at the dustbowl to be confronted with a fleet of CR2 that had had the OPFOR iron cross daubed in red paint all over them. The OC was not a happy man!

The exercise was going fairly well up until my vehicle started to have a few communications issues and in particular problems with the vehicle i/c. On two separate occasions during the live fire phase I lost the ability to speak to the rest of the crew. A number of REME techs investigated the problem but could not find any definite problem with it being an intermittent fault. So, we carried on and hoped for the best. The next serial involved us being used as the assault tanks in a Squadron attack. As we crested the hill and got eyes on to the objective I laid the gunner on to a target which he engaged. I then spotted a further target and satisfied the gunner had destroyed the first one laid him on to the next target. However, in the heat of the moment when I told the gunner to "traverse" right the driver thought he heard "right stick" and started to pull right. I didn't immediately notice as I was looking at the target, but upon having a quick glance out of my episcope to check our balance with the troop leader I realised we were heading towards him and would collide in the not too distant future. I shouted at the driver to pull left stick, but we carried on going right. The i/c was playing up again! I tapped the gunner on the shoulder and shouted at him to stop firing and was screaming at the top of my lungs for the driver to stop. The troop leader had realised what was happening and was bringing his vehicle to a halt. Just prior to impact the driver realised he had not heard anything on the i/c and started to slow down, just in time to reduce the force of the impact as we collided with Callsign 10! After a quick check to make sure that everyone was okay on our own vehicle we opened up and shouted across to make sure the crew on 10 were all okay too. Fortunately, there was not too much damage to either vehicle, a couple of damaged road wheels and bent skirting plates. The biggest damage was to my ego for having had the collision and I had to endure a fair bit of banter from the troop and in turn the rest of the Squadron too. The OC in particular gave me a hard time, but he would come to regret it!

A few days later as we were coming to the end of our live firing phase the Squadron were in a number of blocking positions in anticipation of an enemy advance through our area. The OC had taken the opportunity during a lull to move forward and assess the positions the troops were occupying. It was at this stage that the enemy started to advance, and the OC was a little too sharp for comfort. He decided that a high speed reverse was required, but failed to check that the area behind him was clear!!! As a result, just as the driver had hit 4th gear and a speed of around 25 mph there was a loud bang and the vehicle came to a sudden stop. The OC had reversed his vehicle straight in to the 2nd Troop Sergeants tank. The whole exercise was brought to a halt to see if there were any injuries and what the extent of the vehicle damage was. Whilst my earlier collision had resulted in relatively minor damage to the vehicles involved, the OC managed to write off both CR2 tanks!!! Quite a costly collision!

The troop on the local training area.

THE JOYS OF CAM NETS, CANVAS AND BREAKFAST

On a chilly windswept rainy morning on Soltau, C Squadron stopped to leaguer up in the early hours of the morning. It was still dark and I was the Squadron Leaders gunner. The driver was Terry McConnell and the radio operator/loader was Ken Davidson (KD). The Squadron leader told us to Cam up while he went for an O group. KD was on Radio stag so me and Terry had to put the Cam net up in the pouring rain on our own. It took us over an hour to put the Cam net and bivvy up and we were exhausted, soaked and ready for our sleeping bags when the Squadron Leader, Major Charlie Comyn came back and said, "we are now on 10 minutes notice to move" so the Cam net and Bivvy had to come down and be put away! So, we (Terry and me) set about taking it all down and tidying up whilst the Squadron Leader made his notes in the turret and KD stayed on radio stag! Having taken the Cam net and Bivvy down and stowed everything away the Squadron Leader said he was hungry and asked us to do some breakfast. Terry set up the cooker on the back decks and did a fry up. It has to be said that although Terry was the driver he had taken on the mantle of crew chef and took pride in his cooking and especially the presentation of the meals to the Squadron Leader. So Terry passes me the Squadron Leaders breakfast to pass in to the turret to him when the whole breakfast slid off of the metal plate and on to the back decks. Terry's face was a picture of horror as a very pissed off and soaked Bobby Russell scooped the breakfast, dirt, muck (and engine oil too), back on to the plate saying to Terry, "if he wants his f...ing breakfast he can have it!" Terry tried in vain to stop me passing it in, in a bit of a state, to the Squadron Leader but failed! Terry then hid, dreading what the Squadron Leader might say, but after about 10 minutes the Squadron Leader popped his head out of the Commanders hatch and as he passed me his clean plate he said, "Cpl Russell tell Cpl McConnell that's the best breakfast he's ever made!"

A VITAL OPERATION

Cpl A had decided that two daughters were enough for anyone and that a vasectomy was required. During an initial check it was noted that he was a particularly hairy individual and that he might like to shave a little prior to the operation. Cpl A had not really grasped the meaning and told his best mate, Cpl B what had been said and asked him what had been meant by "shave a little". Cpl B apparently whispered the answer to him. When Cpl A arrived for the operation the doctor conducting the operation burst out laughing. "Cpl A." he said with a broad smile, "who told you to shave from the neck down?"

"FIGHTING C" - HERRICK 15

Captain "Sib" Davidson

In 2011 C Squadron sojourned to Afghanistan in a completely different role than we were used to. We had re-trained as a light role infantry Company for the deployment. Six years later I write this with fond memories of the Officers and Soldiers I had the pleasure to serve with. I am proud to have served with Hussars that showed professionalism, bravery and a stoic determination to get the job done no matter what. If I was to try and put it all down on paper it would take me years, instead I will try and give a brief overview of some of the more memorable events along the way.

In camp training

When it was decided that we would re-role a team from 5 Rifles was sent over to get us in the mood. This small but dedicated team were outstanding. They constantly pushed and strived to get us up to standard and passed on knowledge and experience to all ranks. The lads were constantly on the move. In or out of camp we were relentlessly practicing and rehearsing until drills became a natural reaction. What we didn't know at the time was that some kind soul had arranged for us to have a few weeks booster training with the CSgt's at Brecon.

Brecon

Our training was well under way. Now it was time for troops to have their skills honed by the staff at the Infantry Training Centre, Brecon. This was a couple of weeks in the field based out of an old farm house. The CSgt's introduced the lads to the joys of section attack loops; ankle snapping terrain and mosquito's that could bite you through your body armour.

If anyone ever tells you that it can't rain upwards, then they are lying. As soon as you cross that bloody cattle grid onto the training area it did. We have 140 Hussars that can prove it.

The training culminated in a clearance operation of SILINI village. The boys did a fantastic job and did it with such speed and efficiency that the Infantry Corps RSM turned to our CO and RSM and stated that "They are fit for purpose. "and then stormed off!!!!!

Mission specific training.

These exercises are a test of the sub unit's efficiency. It tests all aspects of training for the upcoming tour. There were several exercises around the UK, from Castlemartin in Wales to Otterburn in Northumberland. It was a real test of the G4 chain moving from Germany to the UK and back again constantly and we became very good at expeditionary deployments and finding what we needed when we needed it!!!! I have never stolen anything, I prefer to liberate items that might be of use..............

UK Customs and Borders Agency

On one of the exercises we had to deploy to Otterburn. Due to the fact that some penny pinching civil servant wanted to save money we had to drive from Sennelager via Calais/Dover to Otterburn. This was a real treat for the G4 team as the Pantecs were restricted to 90km per hour. We set off two days before the rest of the Squadon and they still beat us there!!!

On this journey I had the pleasure of almost causing an international incident. On arrival at the port of Calais we were sent through to the freight departures. We arrived at the check point and I was asked "Do you have any weapons or explosives? " I, being over tired and slightly sarcastic replied "As a matter of fact I do: 150 SA80's, 36 LMG'S, 24 GPMG's and slight dusting of grenade launchers!!" The French blokes face drained of colour! He started shaking and muttering in French on the radio. Next, sirens, security and flashing lights!!!! Once I explained who we were and what we were doing the UK Customs guys calmed things down considerably.

Otterburn

I will never forget this day. I had a text message from SSgt Dickinson saying, "Mate I'm at Otterburn. I've just been told I'm taking over from you as the CQMS?" I replied, "I don't know what you're on about pal". On arrival the OC, Maj Porter called me over and said "You've six hours to handover. You're now the CSM! All I could think was "I've only got a fucking A4 NIREX! "

It seems that everyone else knew what was going on but me and Dicko. Because this was one of the final exercises I was going to be put through the grinder to test my FOB (Forward Operating Base) defence and CASEVAC procedures.

We deployed onto the area and occupied the FOB. After an initial patrol down to the local village we returned. As soon as the last man was through the gate the FOB defence started. Over the next four hours we were attacked constantly and just for good measure the DS threw in 27 casualties to test our skills and drills.

During one particular serial the DS used an actor from a company called 'Amputees in action' (AIA). Some of these guys are former soldiers that have been injured on tour and the simulated injuries they present are very realistic. During one very heavy simulated IDF attack, we had several casualties and due to the on-going FOB defence serial, I had to call the new CQMS and his lads out to help me load them on the helicopter. One of the AIA actors was missing both legs and one arm. He was a former Green Jacket that had been blown up in Northern Ireland during the 80's and he was a real character. As I was counting the casualties onto the helicopter I noticed that one was missing. As I looked round I could see Dicko running across the FOB with him tucked under one arm! As he placed him down in the helicopter on the stretcher in front of the medic the actor looked up and said "He moves quick for a fat lad don't he? Like a human hippo! "Everyone involved in the serial stopped doing what they were doing and burst out laughing.

Afghanistan

Shortly before we were due to deploy the Company was told that we would be split between four locations. I can only cover some events that happened at PB (Patrol Base) ATTAL.

PB ATTAL – CHQ and a bolstered 1PL.
DURIA JUNCTIION – 2 PL.
LASHKARGAH/NIADULLAH – 3PL.

Before we deployed we were briefed that our AOR was in transition and wasn't very kinetic. This as it turns out was incorrect. PB ATTAL was located on the 601 and protected the MSR (Main Supply Route) from Lashkargah to Duria Junction. PB ATTAL housed around 400 soldiers from various units. We had our own integral gun battery, PWRR Recce Pl, engineers, bomb disposal teams, LAD, medics and chefs. The conditions in the camp were not what we expected as all in all it was a nice place to live and operate from.

We conducted many Ops and on several occasions we teamed up with our D Squadron brethren. They were mounted on WARTHOG and I believe this may have been the first time QRH wagons had dropped and picked up QRH dismounts in and out of contact.

During our tour we lost one good man and two others had life changing injuries. By the end of the tour most of us had a grudging respect for the Taliban fighters. Around 47 of them found out that we were pretty good at fighting too!!!

We were also equipped with Jackal and Mastiff vehicles and on one patrol into BGHQ for an O Group I noticed a series of forts along the 601 that Alexander the Great had established when he had invaded Afghanistan. I remember thinking to myself we are doing the exactly the same thing. Would we make the same mistakes?

The 'BERCO' boiler.

Every Ops room should have a BERCO boiler to ensure a constant supply of brews. After tea one night the CQMS was getting ripped for being rubbish because of the lack of constant hot water. The following is only hearsay and rumour.

CQMS Dickinson (Dicko) took his ripping that badly that he allegedly booked himself on a chopper flight back to Camp Bastion. It is then that the alleged liberation of the BERCO took place. Rumour has it that he walked into the cookhouse and unplugged a BERCO and started emptying it. When he was challenged by the civvy contractors as to what he was doing he allegedly produced an unserviceable sign and placed it on the boiler. He then sat down and had his lunch whilst the boiler cooled down. When he had finished his lunch he promptly left with boiler and got on the next flight to PB ATTAL with it.

The KANDAK Sgt Maj

Outside of PB ATTAL was the HQ for the local Police Kandak. I had struck up a friendship with the Sgt Maj based on mutual respect. He was good guy who tried to do the right thing on a difficult day, even when those around him were clearly AT IT!!!

Unfortunately, one day he stood on an IED. As we had a fully functional MRS in PB ATTAL they brought him to the main gate. The main sanger alerted me as to what was going on and I and Guard Commander quickly assessed the situation. The Guard Commander took one look at the wound and promptly stabilised him after applying a tourniquet. We then proceeded to the MRS. They had been informed by the Ops room what was going on. I burst in there and it was all set up for major surgery. The medical staff asked "CSM what's your assessment?" Out of breath and sweating the only thing that came to mind was, "He's fucked! "The Doc was not impressed with my medical assessment!!!

The O Group rant!!!

I'm not proud of this one but it is funny. I had been to BGHQ for the RSM's conference. He had given us very clear direction on the following:

1. Military working dogs are not to be treated as pets.
2. Shaving – must take place when in camp and there is a plentiful supply of water.

I arrived back in ATTAL and immediately noted that some of the lads were throwing the ball for a one of the search dogs. So that evening I let rip at the O Group, ranting on about military working dogs being an asset etc etc. I then moved on to the point on shaving. As I was re-enforcing the topic I spotted someone lurking at the back of the Ops room in the half light. As I looked closer it appeared that they had some stubble around the sideburns and the start of a very poor moustache. Clearly the individual got, "and you! Hiding at the back there! You best get a fucking shave pronto! "

After the O Group I went for a cigarette in the smoking area. It was then that SSgt Fisher informed me that the individual I had just gripped was in fact the new female artillery officer who had just arrived....

The white Toyota Corolla.

"Int indicates" is a saying that comes out on every set of orders. During our tour we seemed to be constantly looking for an elusive white Toyota Corolla which may contain a car bomb.

One day we were told that the CO was coming down to hold a shura with the Kandak Commander and we were told to expect the Taliban to attack the compound. With this in mind, we set the security around the location and we had a heavy presence in the local area to deter them. Once the outside was secure we set up the "eyes on" inside, awaiting the arrival of the CO. When everything was set and the Shura was up and running the RSM and I snuck off for sneaky smoke. We sat on the bonnet of a car with a tarpaulin over it and had a chat about few things. The final point was "I wonder why this car is covered up?"

Let's just say that the Shura ended and we left very quickly whilst the Police Kandak disposed of a huge car bomb they had found.

The HAF – Heliborn assault force.

This operation was one of the most exciting things I have ever done. How we all got back in one piece I will never know. With the OC on R&R it was down to the 2I/C, Capt G Denaro to command the op. Our movement had been stifled due to an IED belt, so it was decided that we needed to put the Taliban on the back foot by hopping behind the belt to conduct a strike operation.

The day came and off we went in two Chinook helicopters with Apaches in support. We landed and de-bussed, set the outer cordon and 41A conducted a strike and search of a couple of compounds. From radio chatter it seemed we were being set up for an ambush.

With the Op complete we moved to HLS 1 and cleared it. We were set and ready to get picked up. As the helicopters approached the Taliban opened up on them and the landing was aborted.

We moved on to the EHLS (Emergency Helicopter Landing Site) and cleared that. We called the Chinooks back in. The multiples were lined up in good order. As the Chinooks landed the Taliban opened up from several firing points. The guys peeled out and returned fire. As the lads were moving you could see the strike of the bullets in the mud all around us. We had to peel onto the helicopter returning fire as we went.

Not to be outdone the Chinook crews opened up with their miniguns. The compound that we had been contacted from actually collapsed before our eyes. Very impressive indeed.

The building of Check Point MIR AGHA.

In order to try and take some ground back it was decided that we would build and occupy a check point near a village called

Purpalzay. This village had been and was being used as a staging post for the Taliban for shoot and scoots and was riddled with IED's. It was a lovely little back water that was once described by Captain Gareth Prince to the Joint Chiefs of Staff as, "you don't want to go in there. It's a little bit fighty".

The day arrived, and it was like an OPTAG serial from hell. We deployed and were dropped off by D Squadron in the WARTHOGS. As we entered the compound we found a woman having a baby in one of the huts. As we were dealing with that the lorry carrying the ISO container with the engineer equipment required for the build slipped off the road and the ISO popped off its brackets. Between us we came up with the idea of using one of the winches off a Jackal to pop it back in place.

With the occupants of the compound now finally ready to leave they loaded up their tractor which promptly fell off the bridge next to the compound. This task was becoming a real treat!!!

With day one out of the way we set to it. For the next ten days or so we re-enforced the walls, built a Super Sanger and humped and dumped an untold amount of gravel into the Hesco we had brought with us. All the while there were sporadic small arms contacts as the Taliban tried to stop us securing the location. They even tried to flood us out!!!!

To top it off, when we had finished the engineers had a little surprise for us. They had built the chicane at the main gate so small that we couldn't get the bloody vehicles out!

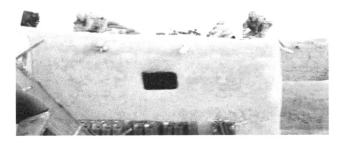

Slightly out of focus shot of the lads diving for cover during the build. The lad on the left is Tpr Hall. He shouted down at me "Sir, there shooting at us! "My reply was, "Well fucking shoot back then kiddo!"

Inside the completed build. The vehicles are Jackals

EPILOGUE – THE RANT

We have come to the end of our compilation. I am very grateful to all that contributed to this book. I believe it gives an inkling of the soldier in the 20th century and a good picture of what the soldier faces in the 21st century. It shows that throughout the time frame covered, the Queen's Hussars, be they Queen's Own, Queen's Royal Irish or Queen's Royal have been second to none, have set standards that have not been bettered and at times have achieved what many thought could not be achieved. The Regiment of today maintains those standards and traditions well and carries them into the future.

The Army of today is vastly different from the Army I joined in 1974. It has 80000 fewer soldiers, considerably less armour, artillery and aviation and much of that is obsolete. There are some good bits of kit and there are some pretty useless items if we are to fight another conventional war. The Army faces challenges of peace keeping and peace making. The great Russian bear is still on the doorstep and still acting like a territorial grizzly. It continues to try and fight proxy wars against the west. These threats are all real, but they are perhaps not the greatest threats. The greatest threats may be political correctness, an insidious erosion of standards and the insistence that contracting out is better than in house provision.

There have been some great improvements in how we manage our soldiers. No longer is being taken to the rear of a vehicle and thumped considered an acceptable form of discipline. Career management is conducted with much more rigour and living conditions for both single and married soldiers have improved. However, there are now other issues to be faced. Women in the front line, equality and homosexuality. These are all easily manageable. Provided discipline is applied fairly to both men and women and that discipline is justifiable then "Get on with it."

It will be a challenge to the Commanding Officer and members of the Warrant Officers and Sergeants Mess to maintain the self-respect and discipline of soldiers in an age when "Equality" and

"Fair Treatment" can mean there is a fear of offending anyone about anything. Soldiers will still be required to go "over the top!" be they male or female or even "gender neutral" and to do that they must have self-respect, discipline and pride in the Regiment and their comrades. The people who are best able to influence these qualities on the shop floor are the Warrant Officers and Sergeants who must be the cream of the Regiment.

The Army (and other services) must be wary of the application of civilian standards and law to the military. Soldiers are very different creatures to civilians (trust me. I am finding out how different now I am retired.). They are asked to do things that would make many civilians blanche. The vast majority of civilians have no understanding of what it means to be a soldier and face the threats that our servicemen do. Soldiers need a style of leadership and camaraderie that is beyond politicians. Our senior Officers must not become political beasts. They must be apolitical and fight any imposition of standards and law that make the soldiers job more dangerous. Commanding Officers and RSMs must familiarise themselves with new instructions and apply them in the way that suits the soldier. Standards that ensure self-respect and Esprit de Corps must be fought for and maintained unless they are replaced by something better.

Many of the reductions in Army strength have been contracted out. Babcocks, Huntings, Defence Support Group, Carillion (oops), Sodexho and others all perform duties soldiers used to perform. Financially for the government good news as pension pots do not have to be filled and the wages bill is reduced. However, in the search for further savings manpower is easy to chop and one of the first elements of that manpower that has gone are those who were monitoring the contracts. This gives a free hand to contractors to self audit and make money hand over fist. You may recall the shock and horror of the news in 2012 when it was revealed that a contractor changing a lightbulb cost something in the region of a hundred pounds. The excuse was that the contractor had to employ a person to change the bulb, give him transport to get to the job, set up the administrative staff and systems to log the job and accountants to charge the MOD and all of these needed paying for. Well, no kidding Batman! For all those bright officers and civil servants in MOD, before a contract is finally signed there must be a review of the processes that the contractor is going to use to meet the contract. Those processes should be written down legally and clearly. The contract must then be monitored on a regular basis because if it is not and the contractor decides to do something differently it is only a matter of months before that becomes legal and there is the square root of nothing that can be done about it without going through the change contract process, which costs money.

The final and Real and Present Danger is being constantly based in one UK location. There is discussion about the number of quarters being reduced and soldiers renting properties at market rates. There is risk that the military "family" (that includes the wife of the soldier) becomes split and that it becomes impossible to support that family. Currently whilst the majority of families are in quarters in a close knit society the families can help to support each other during a deployment. It is relatively easy to get families in for briefings and to keep them informed. This is not the case if those families are spread to the four winds, in civilian accommodation amongst people who have no idea what that family is going through when spouses and partners are deployed. Ask the reserves that deploy. Whatever happens, Commanding Officers and Squadron Leaders must always remember that the families suffer as much, if not more than the soldiers during a deployment and the build up to it. At least the soldiers have constant company. Families are the life blood of the Regiment and must be treated as such, regardless of where the Regiment is based and where those families live. NCO's and Officers must know the families of their soldiers.

Finally, serving soldiers and Officers deserve the support of all Old Comrades, regardless of capbadge. The serving regiment maintains the traditions and standards of the Regiments we all loved.

Lightning Source UK Ltd.
Milton Keynes UK
UKHW051603160322
400080UK00007B/116